THE STATES
AND THE METROPOLIS

PUBLIC ADMINISTRATION AND PUBLIC POLICY

A Comprehensive Publication Program

Executive Editor

JACK RABIN

Graduate Program for Administrators
Rider College
Lawrenceville, New Jersey

Publications in Public Administration and Public Policy

1. Public Administration as a Developing Discipline (in two parts)
   by Robert T. Golembiewski
2. Comparative National Policies on Health Care
   by Milton I. Roemer, M.D.
3. Exclusionary Injustice: The Problem of Illegally Obtained Evidence
   by Steven R. Schlesinger
4. Personnel Management in Government: Politics and Process
   by Jay M. Shafritz, Walter L. Balk, Albert C. Hyde, and David H. Rosenbloom
5. Organization Development in Public Administration (in two parts)
   edited by Robert T. Golembiewski and William B. Eddy
6. Public Administration: A Comparative Perspective
   Second Edition, Revised and Expanded
   by Ferrel Heady
7. Approaches to Planned Change (in two parts)
   by Robert T. Golembiewski
8. Program Evaluation at HEW (in three parts)
   edited by James G. Abert
9. The States and the Metropolis
   by Patricia S. Florestano and Vincent L. Marando
10. Personnel Management in Government: Politics and Process (second edition, revised and expanded)
    by Jay M. Shafritz, Albert C. Hyde, and David H. Rosenbloom

Other volumes in preparation

THE STATES AND THE METROPOLIS

Patricia S. Florestano
Vincent L. Marando

The University of Maryland
College Park, Maryland

MARCEL DEKKER, INC.   New York and Basel

Library of Congress Cataloging in Publication Data

Florestano, Patricia S.
 The states and the metropolis.

 (Public administration and public policy ; 9)
 Includes bibiographical references and index.
 1. State-local relations--United States.
I. Marando, Vincent L. , [date]. II. Title.
III. Series.
 JS348. F6   353. 9'293   81-5526
 ISBN 0-8247-1287-0   AACR2

COPYRIGHT © 1981 by MARCEL DEKKER, INC. ALL RIGHTS RESERVED

Neither this book nor any part may be reproduced or transmitted in any form or by any means, electronic or mechanical, including photocopying, microfilming, and recording, or by any information storage and retrieval system, without permission in writing from the publisher.

MARCEL DEKKER, INC.
270 Madison Avenue, New York, New York 10016

Current printing (last digit):
10 9 8 7 6 5 4 3 2 1

PRINTED IN THE UNITED STATES OF AMERICA

Preface

The purpose of our study is to examine how states relate to their local governments which are situated in metropolitan areas and, specifically, how they relate to the urban environment as it undergoes metropolitanization. Metropolitanization is a dynamic process that is occurring throughout the nation, and we seek to determine the amount of attention states are giving to this process and what direction such attention is taking.

Our perspective is that of supporters of reform in government. But as reformers we are somewhat skeptical about the real impact of much of the activity we are witnessing at the state level. We agree that states are now more concerned about their localities; and we agree that there is now more state action concerning local needs. But we are less certain about the overall direction of this activity and the overall policy planning behind it. We are, for example, curious regarding the amount of state activity specifically targeted on the needs of distressed areas and people.

We shall try to answer some of these questions in this study through conscientious evaluation of state government activities. In doing so, we hope to convey, to scholars and students alike, a sense of the dynamics of the metropolitanization that is taking place across our country and of the rich potential that resides in our states.

Patricia S. Florestano
Vincent L. Marando

Contents

Preface	iii
1 / THE STATES AND THE METROPOLIS	1
Introduction	1
States and Urban Areas	3
Nation, States, and Localities: A Point of Reference	4
The States and Urban Areas: Various Perspectives	6
Notes	14
2 / METROPOLITANIZATION	16
Introduction	16
An Organization of Space	17
Governmental Decentralization in the Metropolis	28
The Nature of Community in Metropolitan Areas	31
States and Metropolitan Areas: An Overview	33
Notes	35
3 / THE STATES, FEDERALISM, AND HOME RULE	37
Introduction	37
The Web of Government	37
Interdependencies of Governments and the Sharing of Power	41
The State's Pivotal Role in Federalism	42
State Constitutions - Localities as Communities	50
Competence of Government: States	51
Notes	54
4 / LOCAL GOVERNMENT FORMS AND FUNCTIONS	56
Introduction	56
Local Government in a State Context	56
Types of Local Government	57

Structural and Boundary Changes in Local Government 65
Procedural Changes: State-Initiated 79
Conclusion 82
Notes 82

5 / FINANCING LOCAL GOVERNMENTS IN METROPOLITAN AREAS 86
Introduction 86
Revenues: Local Sources 87
Expenditures 95
Contrasts in Metropolitan Communities 103
State Limitations on Local Revenues 104
State Aid 106
State Fiscal Decisions and Future Directions 112
Notes 114

6 / STATE LAND-USE POLICY 117
Introduction 117
State Land Use: The Issues and Interests 119
States' Reentry into Land-Use Policy 120
State Involvement: No Panacea 124
State Land-Use Approaches 129
Notes 135

7 / STATE DEVELOPMENT OF URBAN-METROPOLITAN STRATEGIES 137
Introduction 137
State Departments of Community Affairs 138
State Commissions on Local Government 140
Federal and State Urban Strategy 149
Conclusions 151
Notes 152

8 / THE STATES AND THE METROPOLITAN AREAS: RESEARCH, ISSUES, AND THE FUTURE 154
Introduction 154
Research Themes 155
The Federal Context 157
Notes 160

Index 163

Chapter 1

THE STATES AND THE METROPOLIS

INTRODUCTION

The United States continues to urbanize. As the most urban nation in the world, it is developing urban space by means of the most sophisticated technologies available and mobilizing vast resources to shape its metropolises. In this continuing process of urbanization, conscious public policy does not remain the exclusive province of any single level of government. Instead, all levels of government--local, state, and national--as well as the private sector have some impact on urban problems.

Governmental functions and policies to deal with urban problems have never been the divining rod for determining a division of powers among the various governmental entities. Like the powers, resources, and needs of governments, the relationships among governmental units have been in constant flux. To grasp what policies have been attempted and might be pursued in confronting the needs of urban areas is to come to grips with the complexities of policy formulation in the United States. An assessment of urban areas which unilaterally focuses only upon localities, the national government, or the states will be a seriously limited approach.

To study urban political phenomena is to study federalism and intergovernmental relationships. The perspective taken in any assessment of urban areas depends upon the frame of reference of the observers and is an arbitrary decision to be supported by the rationale of the authors. Although we acknowledge that urban areas are responsive to many "levels" of governments and the private sector, we give primacy to the states and to their relationship to the metropolis. We do so in order to untangle the complex of governmental activities and because we believe that states can have the most effect on urban areas if they choose to act. By examining states, which occupy the strategic middle ground in the federal system, we can assess the constraints on localities and the national government in their dealings with urban areas. We will therefore argue that states are the "level" of government which can shape the intergovernmental activities that impact urban areas. Although federal aid to cities has been on the increase, many governmental activities lie substantially beyond the reach of the federal government. Local governmental organization, taxation power, and land use control, for example, are beyond federal control. The ground rules for local action in these areas are laid down by the states, and it is therefore the states that will receive our greatest attention.

We will not argue that states can be the salvation of urban areas nor that they are the cause of most of the problems that beset the metropolis. Localities are always influenced by state actions or inactions, and we will therefore stress in this volume the states' potential to utilize this influence by focusing on the opportunities and constraints they may encounter in dealing with urban issues.

We recognize that there are fifty states and that they differ significantly in how they assist and relate to localities. There is a great deal of documentation that all states have made progress in assisting urban areas. However, our major concern will not be in cataloging all the strides states have made during the last two decades. States have changed and are dynamic. We want to know the direction states are taking in regard to their metropolitan areas. Thus we focus upon whether states have a thematic policy for relating to urban areas, and we will examine what states want to accomplish. We look at the priorities that states have established and we study the posture of states toward urban areas.

A central thesis we present in this volume is that there is a pronounced difference between cities and metropolitan areas. They are not synonymous. The city is a legal creature of the state, granted a charter of incorporation specifying its authority and obligations. The metropolis is a social, economic, and cultural area which contains central cities, suburban municipalities, and the urbanizing fringe. The metropolis is not a governmental entity which states have created. We will demonstrate that the metropolis is in fact the artifact of a definable process which is occurring in all states. We believe that understanding the metropolis and its process of evolution, which we will refer to as metropolitanization, is the context for discussing the state role. Out of metropolitanization flow many of the opportunities and problems that confront urban areas. It is this relationship between states and the metropolis that we examine.

STATES AND URBAN AREAS

Throughout the past two decades, the question of the role to be played by the various levels of government in urban areas has been a critical issue. During the 1960s, and until quite recently, the states were viewed as being the weakest governmental links in dealing with urban issues. Representative of this view is Roscoe Martin's statement that "the states have a traditional responsibility for the cities and their problems, but few would maintain that they have discharged that responsibility in anything approaching satisfactory fashion. The federal government reveals both a growing awareness to bring national resources to bear in seeking their abatement, though it remains to be seen what results federal participation will produce."[1]

These results of national participation have since been assessed by Arthur Naftalin and Reynold Boezi: "By now it is clear that the many federal efforts designed to help American cities have had, at best, limited effectiveness. We are in a season of critical re-examination of what went wrong and are perhaps beginning to understand why the many federal programs for urban areas fall short of expectations."[2] Some observers felt that the federal government in the Great Society era had thrown money at urban problems with the consequence of setting up cities for a crisis that broke out a few years later.[3]

This reassessment of the roles of the national and state governments in urban areas is corroborated in the National Urban Policy. President Jimmy Carter's Urban and Regional Policy Group Report reflects the current awareness among political leaders which shape the intergovernmental partnership context for urban areas. In fact, the report was titled "A New Partnership to Conserve America's Communities." The partnership was to include the states as one of the primary partners.[4] The report acknowledges that until recently, the federal government has shown little interest in the role states might play in developing and carrying out national urban policies and asserts that the states are often in the best position to solve some of our urban problems. The federal government has bypassed the states on many occasions and has dealt directly with localities. But fiscal and social problems resulting from political fragmentation in urban areas can be resolved only at the state capital. Only the state can balance municipal responsibilities and resources; and only on the state level can new regional and metropolitan approaches be developed for providing services and balancing resources among cities and fringe areas.[5]

The states' powers to effect changes in urban areas are often categorized as they were in the National Urban Policy, covering the creation of local government, the ability to determine state and local tax rates, jurisdiction over land use, power to regulate and establish environmental standards, and numerous other categories. The states have had these powers since the creation of the nation. The recognition that these powers can be used to address urban problems and the hope that they will be is the theme of the 1980s. However, this hope for the states' role may prove no more realistic than did the enthusiasm for national involvement in the 1960s. Thus, we recognize that the observations presented in this volume are bound by many constraints upon states which are not acknowledged. Despite the states' great potential, there is still no consensus among scholars and policymakers as to what they can actually accomplish.

NATION, STATES, AND LOCALITIES: A POINT OF REFERENCE

Few observers of the American political system would deny that the states have authority over their localities. All powers exercised by local governments to levy taxes, provide services, and enact ordinances are granted by the states. According to "Dillon's rule," named after the Iowa justice who originally decided the case, all forms of local governmental units are created by the state, and it is the state which delegates power to localities.[6] The states have the power to regulate the actions of local governments, and, if necessary, state authority can be employed to dissolve, abolish, and reorganize local governmental entities.

Dillon's rule was enunciated over a century ago. It has been tested many times in state and federal courts, including the Supreme Court of the United States, and continues to be the guiding principle governing the legal status of local government.[7] In the absence of a state constitutional grant or guarantee, local governments have no authority independent from that granted by state law. Legally, local governmental units are created by and dependent upon the state.

The United States Constitution makes no reference to local government. It was assumed that localities would be the responsibility of and within the authority of the states. This is not to imply that the federal government has no dealings with local governments. In fact, quite the opposite is true. Many federal programs are designed to bypass the states and give financial resources directly to local governments. The General Revenue Sharing Program is a recent testimony of federal aid being given to local governments. Approximately two-thirds of all federal general revenue funds, which amount to about

$5 billion annually, goes directly to general-purpose local governments. The remaining one-third goes to states.

The federal assistance that goes directly to local governments reflects the political power localities have brought to bear upon Congress and the president. Observers of the American political scene now recognize that localities have exerted pressure upon and received aid from the national government since the beginning of our federal system. The extent of federal assistance to localities was enlarged by the Great Depression when the federal government was the only governmental unit with resources to assist localities. Federal aid to localities has been escalated during the late 1960s and 1970s, to the point where local governments have become "dependent" on federal resources.[8] T. D. Allman indicates that federal aid has increased so massively during the past decade that it accounts for half of the total revenues in several cities. The increase in federal aid was extremely rapid. In the two decades from 1958 to 1978, federal aid increased tenfold from less than 5% of cities' general revenue to about half.

David B. Walker of the Advisory Commission on Intergovernmental Relations (ACIR) says that currently a panoramic concept of partnership is emerging that now includes the federal government and practically all local governments and, of course, the states.[9] Walker goes on to make two other important points about the significance of increasing federal aid to localities. First, approximately 30% of the total federal aid to cities and counties bypasses state governments. Second, there has also been such a steady proliferation of federal aid programs that hardly any governmental activity at the local level is not covered by some federal grant. The federal government deluges localities with hundreds of specialized programs as well as the "no strings" General Revenue Sharing funds. The federal-local relationships are multiple and complex and the states are active partners in only some of the programs.

Although local governments are not even mentioned in the United States Constitution, they have, in reality, become a third element in the federal system, alongside national and state governments. At this point, local governments are the benefactors of more programs and receive more federal aid than at any time in the nation's history. It is within this context of multiple and massive federal-local linkages that the role of state governments in urban areas is being reassessed.

The state's role and the complex of intergovernmental relations in the United States has been classically formulated by Morton Grodzins.[10] His fundamental notion, which continues to be the accepted view, is that the American system of government of shared activities and services is functionally analogous to a marble cake even though it is formally structured in three planes like a layer cake. All "levels" and programs are intermixed and difficult to separate out among the separate "layers" of government. Although more recent analogies liken the federal system to a picket fence built along functional grants and aid lines from federal to state to local, or to rubber bands which stretch to accommodate various pressures and conflicts but do not lose their basic shape, none seriously depicts the system as three truly separate levels of government.

Grodzins further argued that the American federal system has never really been a system of separated governmental activities. He documented the fact that there has never been a time when it was possible to put distinct labels on discrete "federal," "state," and "local" functions. Historically, the system of shared activities among the levels of government existed even before the adoption of the Constitution, and the levels were always intertwined in providing the basic governmental functions. Although the relative impact of the three levels of government on urban dwellers has varied over time and according to function, there has been no period in the American history when local government concerns were purely local or state government was confined solely to state functions. Further, national policies and programs continue to be administered primarily through the states and localities.

Thus it is quite difficult to discuss state or local governments without making reference to interrelationships among them and with the national government. The shaping of power in the United States is exercised through complex arrangements of structures which vary according to the activity under consideration. The national government's tremendous growth since the Depression is well recognized: apart from its dominance in foreign policy, it has become dominant in many areas of domestic policy as well. States continue largely to fund and regulate education, highways, and several other areas, while localities determine most issues of land use. Depending upon the governmental activity, the mix of influence of the various "levels" of governments varies. To disentangle this web of interrelationship across all activities in order to examine strictly state influences is indeed a difficult task.

THE STATES AND URBAN AREAS: VARIOUS PERSPECTIVES

There are three points which are central to understanding state impact in urban areas. First, there must be an objective assessment of the endemic problems to be addressed. Second, there also must be some criterion or standard against which the states' efforts can be evaluated.

Third, to guide analysis of states' policies for urban areas, there must be some theory or perspective of state involvement and policy impact on urban issues. Let us take up these three points individually.

Urban Problems

Urban problems are moving targets. They include a wide spectrum of social, economic, political, and physical problems. Their severity varies significantly within our metropolitan areas. Many central cities are inhabited by the poor and by minorities who do not have resources sufficient to meet their needs. City governments with declining tax bases find it exceedingly difficult to provide the services required by their residents. On the other hand, many suburban areas are homes of middle- and upper-income groups and have fewer problems with financial support of service delivery. Both cities and suburban areas are touched by problems of declining environmental quality and inadequate transportation networks. The urban problem consists of many subproblems which affect populations to different extents while large proportions of the residents feel that problems do not exist.

There has been a pronounced shift in opinions during the last decade as to whether an urban crisis exists and how severe it is if one does exist. During the 1960s, there was a widespread belief that an urban crisis did exist and that the problems of cities were severe and wide-ranging, from deep-seated racism to the deterioration of the quality of the environment. A representative statement of the urban crisis as depicted in the late 1960s was set forth in <u>The Roles of the States in Solving Urban Problems:</u>

> Almost daily, the American citizen sees, hears, or reads about the "urban crisis." Or he may be a living or half-dead participant in the crisis as he tries to survive in a slum area—perhaps illiterate, perhaps hungry, perhaps ill-housed, unemployed, on narcotics or welfare—or worse. He feels the crisis. . . . We have a litany of problems that beset the suburbanite and the city dweller. . . . We are dealing with a wide spectrum of social, economic, political, psychological, physical and other problems, and with virtually all the institutions of our society.[11]

The Report of the Commission on the Cities in the 1970s echoed a similar concern over the severe problems facing America's large urban areas. Early 1971, three-and-a-half years after the tragic summer of 1967 when many cities were torn with riots, and almost three years since the publication of the Report of the National Advisory Commission on Civil Disorders reexamined the problems of the cities, very little had been achieved in curing urban ills.[12] The Commission on the Cities in the 1970s found that despite the widely accepted Kerner finding that one major cause of the ghetto disorders of the 1960s was the shameful conditions of life in the cities, most of the changes in those conditions since 1968-- at least in the cities the commission visited--were worse.[13] The commission concluded that those who held the power that governs the Unived States did not indicate that they were willing to take the drastic action necessary to make American cities livable again.

The view that America's urban areas are in serious trouble is not universally accepted. Edward Banfield, a leading urbanologist, argued that the problems of cities are not of a critical nature, but merely inconveniences for most.[14] In the activist consciousness-raising period of the decade spanning the late 1960s and 1970s, his book *The Unheavenly City*, with its advocacy of inaction, was regarded as outrageous by many urban activists and scholars. Banfield argued rather gratuitously that all cities today are much better and healthier places to live than were cities of the 1800s. He wrote that apparent urban problems are either (1) solvable except for political barriers; (2) unsolvable because they are inherently unsolvable, as with poverty or with class inadequacies; or (3) not problems at all, as with congestion, which is simply caused by the presence of a great many people and is unavoidable in today's cities. Thus, when it seems that action may be politically unacceptable or may exacerbate the problems it was designed to ameliorate, inaction becomes the policy.

Nevertheless, some students of urban areas say that the distribution of problems within metropolitan areas is spread unevenly and that they do not constitute a single ubiquitous metropolitan problem.[15] They contend that many areas of the metropolis, especially the affluent suburbs, are not confronted with serious urban problems. The urban problem is not governmental fragmentation, poverty, or pollution; rather, the problem exists only in the eyes of the beholders. It is not the residents who perceive urban crises; rather, it is the planners, scholars, and urban experts who define urban environments as in crisis and attempt to convince residents and policymakers that such is the case.

More recent assessments of the "urban problem" indicate that we may have confused the extent of the real problems and spent massive resources on urban problems that could not be resolved. T. D. Allman contends that the real crisis in American cities is that the federal government keeps taking much more out of cities than it puts back.[16] A large portion of federal aid to cities is utterly wasted so far as solving inner city social, economic, and fiscal problems is concerned. An enormous amount of aid goes to people and neighborhoods that do not need help at all. Meanwhile, much of the money that actually reaches inner cities and people in distress does not serve to strengthen their economic base and create work but rather just makes them permanently dependent on such aid. Federal aid to urban areas does absolutely nothing to revive inner-city school systems or to preserve municipal infrastructures, ranging from bridges to sewers, which are deteriorating at an alarming rate. Little measurable effect of vase amounts of federal aid on urban problems has been conclusively documented.

Our purpose here is not to enjoin the debate as to whether an urban crisis exists. We raise the question only as a backdrop for the issue of how and to what extent states can influence urban environments. Can states be more effective in dealing with urban-related issues? We believe this perspective is much more important in the long run than an argument over the existence of a crisis. There may be an intellectual crisis rather than an urban crisis as to what governments, including the state, can effect. As Jerome Zukosky contends, the core problem in the "urban crisis" is the lack of realistic understanding about how governmental institutions work.[17] There is a lack of understanding of how metropolitanization affects local governments' ability to deliver services and the types of services that governments do provide. There are intricate relationships between localities and states about which little concerning the effects of metropolitanization is well known.

State laws are at the heart of resolving defined metropolitan problems, and states do have the authority to make fundamental changes in laws that could effect such solutions. Kolesar specifies these as (1) specifying the internal workings of urban tax systems; (2) setting conditions that determine cost and use of land; and (3) determining the content of basic services.[18] The state may consider altering these structures in order to bring about a better physical environment and better human services delivery system in urban areas. The state's capacity as well as its authority to deal with urban issues is the measure by which to evaluate the capacity of states to govern.

States: Stumbling Blocks or Keystones?

Few scholars deny the potential of states to assist localities in dealing with urban problems. But the translation of that potential into coherent state action has involved a great deal of debate among observers of states. State efforts in assisting urban areas have been criticized as being minimal and of little impact in meeting the needs of cities. At the same time, states have been touted by other observers as the "keystones" of any concerted effort of national, state, and local approach to addressing the needs of urban areas. This difference of opinion about states will continue to exist because much of how states are viewed is a reflection of specific examples of state failures and successes. There is little systematic assessment of all fifty states and their policies for the aid of cities and their residents.

For many years the states have been severely criticized as being the weakest link and most backward level of government in the American political system. Some scholars have depicted the states as that part of the governmental system which performed least well.[19] In their view, the localities have often strained their tax bases and provided additional services to combat some of the problems of their areas, while the states have neither committed adequate resources nor provided the needed leadership. Instead, states have continued their traditional practices and have not responded to the new dimensions of urbanization and metropolitanization. William Colman argues that some--quite a bit--of this castigation has been justified.[20] He indicates that for several decades in the nineteenth century, state governments were noted mainly for the breadth of their collective economic plundering and the depth of their individual financial irresponsibility until an outraged citizenry in a few short years following the Civil War so stripped them of their initiative and so restricted their powers that they have not yet recovered fully.

Charles Press and Charles Adrian have diagnosed the states as being sick. They have argued that states are dominated by a small-town ideology which posits that cities are not the environment in which to find what is best in the American culture. State legislators reflect and reward small-town values and are biased against cities which are considered to represent the worst of modern American culture.[21] Press and Adrian's diagnosis predated the effects of the legislative reapportionment of state legislatures according to the contemporary population trends, as a result of which cities, and even more so suburbs, gained in representation. The effects of reapportionment on the states' responsiveness to the needs of urban areas are now beginning to be felt. State government may no longer be "sick," but the extent to which states have clearly identifiable urban policies has yet to be realized.

To accuse states of being sick and to expect them to accomplish what the federal and local governments cannot accomplish is to "malign" states, according to Ira Sharkansky. He argues that states have accomplished a great deal for their urban areas.[22] Local governments have developed their own constituencies and power bases that often can and do stop state actions which affect them. Although Sharkansky is convinced that states have a better record than their critics are willing to concede, he indicates that the urban benefits from state programs lie as much in the category of potential as in accomplishment.[23]

Moreover, Paul Ylvisaker contends that the states are beginning to make their presence felt in the struggle to shore up local governments that are being battered by the urban tide.[24] Ylvisaker points to the creation of state agencies of community affairs in forty-two states which act as a means by which states can provide a coherent set of services and assistance to localities. Ylvisaker is encouraged that states are recognizing the problems of urban government and that many states are creating programs and machinery to enable them to act. Norman Beckman and Page L. Ingraham also suggest that the states have great potential to play a crucial and positive role in urban areas.[25] They argue that several factors contribute to the state involvement in urban areas. Among these are increases in urbanization which would provide pressure for state involvement and reapportionment of state legislatures which gives more representation to urban areas. Beckman and Ingraham cite a number of examples where states have pursued expanded roles in regional planning, water resources, and tax resources.

Daniel J. Elazar has taken a broad-ranged view of the role of the states in the American federal system.[26] Elazar believes that states are the keystones in the federal system. They play a role which sometimes enables them to function as the fulcrums of governmental activity and at other times as mediators in federal-state-local relations. He has further argued that "a quiet revolution" has transformed state government, as it transformed local government in the 1950s, into a solid instrument for meeting the complex needs of American society today.[27] He concludes that today there is simply no justification for thinking that the states and localities, either in principle or practice, are less able to do the job than the federal government.

Those in the middle of the argument of whether states are stumbling blocks or keystones, such as Jeanne and David Walker, assert that if the states are to be the "middlemen with muscle," not merely "middlemen with potential," their sometimes acrimonious relationships with their localities must be reviewed, revitalized, and in many instances, reformed.[28] State-local relations today are significantly better than they were a decade ago, thanks largely to the activism of states. The Walkers also say that the acid test of the states' real strength lies in their relationship with their own localities which has not been fully realized as of yet.[29]

The point is that the argument can be made both ways. The states may indeed be the weak link in the federal system, but many have made striking commitments to assist local areas. Numerous examples can be cited of the maturing state involvement in local government. But these examples are just that--instances where a certain state accomplished something. There is little overall pattern in what the fifty states are accomplishing in metropolitan areas with respect to urban phenomena generally. Spending more money on higher water-quality standards may be important; at the same time, such an action may not necessarily be a part of a state strategy toward metropolitanization. We take the view that an assessment of state activities can only be made after looking at all states to ascertain the general conditions and trends. Isolated incidents of successes and failure are not a sufficient test. In addition, the strategy that states pursue provides the perspective with which to contrast the separate state actions.

Analytical Perspective

The states occupy the strategic middle between the federal and local governments. States are essential to the functioning of the whole system of American government. Little domestic policy is possible without the cooperation of the states, and if urban problems are to be resolved, the states must be actively engaged. The states have essential control over the "ground rules" that determine the success or failure of major federal urban policies. Determining "ground rules" implies that states possess the power in the "strategic middle" to influence the national government and localities.

Though the states are political entities, as well as mechanisms for federal programs, the great increase in federal aid to urban areas, especially during the New Deal era of the 1930s and the vast expansion of federal programs in the 1970s, has not in fact made the states junior partners in the American political system. The states have remained an overlooked reservoir of political power which affects both federal programs and local activities.

There is much existing and potential power associated with states "being in the middle" of a complex federal system. As Harvey Mansfield noted, the states pervade all areas of domestic policy, performing "some part of almost everything and the whole of very little."[30] We therefore agree with Alan Rosenbaum who argues that in reality states may be the most powerful partner in the federal system.[31] The rationale for this is that states are able to exert great influence over federal funds which "they do not raise." Similarly, as states provide resources to local units of government they shape local policies as well.[32]

Relative to national and local power in urban areas, the states' power base in these areas is also enhanced by several other factors. Many federal programs which affect urban areas pass through and are administered by the state. As has been clearly recognized by policy analysts, the administration of programs carries with it many opportunities to shape and affect them.[33] Federal funds are often intermingled with state resources so that it is difficult to distinquish an independent federal effect in many programs. State political systems are not neutral administrative structures that respond with no isolated policy consequences. State policymakers, both elected and appointed, exert a great deal of influence upon both federal and local governments. What is not clear at this time is the extent or consequences of state policy efforts.

The states have extensive authority and power in several policy areas which affect urban areas. States have preeminent leverage on how local governments are organized--the rules and laws which apply to local governments--and how land is to be used, and states exert great influence on the financing of local governments. States have traditionally aided both urban and rural areas with funds primarily dispersed along functional lines. Approximately 85% of all state expenditures goes for the big three functions of education, highways, and welfare. Aid to general-purpose governments goes to all governments, large and small alike. State assistance to localities is massive and covers many functions and governmental units. What has been lacking at the state level is an urban strategy to guide these vast resources of power. It should be noted also that until March 1978 the federal government had no explicit urban policy. Strategies to deal with metropolitanization are quite recent in both the states and the federal government. Many observers still contend that neither the states nor the federal government have a clear notion of what an urban policy is to accomplish for the nation's metropolitan areas.

The broader point to be stressed is that urban policy is still a relatively fluid and underdeveloped policy area for both the federal and state governments. We contend that it is the state level which can exert vast influence upon metropolitan areas and that the state role has been largely ignored and unanalyzed. Our analysis will start with a discussion of the process of metropolitanization and its effects, because we believe that an understanding of metropolitanization is fundamental to understanding the opportunities and limits of state involvement. We proceed next to examine the context within which states and communities function. Then the three areas in which states have great leverage--local governmental organization, urban fiscal issues, and urban land use--will be examined. This analysis will be followed by a discussion of how states have attempted to pursue an integrated urban policy and will conclude by assessing the direction states are taking in dealing with metropolitan areas.

NOTES

1. Roscoe C. Martin, The Cities and the Federal System (New York: Atherton Press, 1965), p. 18.
2. Arthur Naftalin and Reynold Boezi, "Encouraging Metropolitan Regionalism: A Proposed Federal Initiative," National Urban Policy Round Table Discussion Paper, Project of the Charles F. Kettering Foundation, Columbus, Ohio, January 1978.
3. T. D. Allman, "The Urban Crisis Leaves Town," Harper's, December 1978, pp. 41-56.
4. The President's Urban and Regional Policy Group Report, A New Partnership to Conserve America's Communities (Washington, D.C., March 1978).
5. Ibid., 3:7-8.
6. City of Clinton v. Cedar Rapids and Missouri River Railroad Company, 24 Iowa (1868).
7. Martin, The Cities and the Federal System, p. 30.
8. Allman, "The Urban Crisis Leaves Town," p. 46.
9. David B. Walker, "Local and Federal Aid under the Intergovernmental System," National Civic Review 68, no. 1 (1979): 15-23.
10. Morton Grodzins, in The American System, ed. Daniel J. Elazar (Chicago: Rand McNally, 1966).
11. Center for Urban Social Science Research, The Role of the States in Solving Urban Problems (New Brunswick, N.J.: Rutgers University Press, 1969), p. 1.
12. Fred R. Harris and John V. Lindsay, The State of the Cities (New York: Praeger, 1972), p. 4.
13. Ibid.
14. Edward Banfield, The Unheavenly City (Boston: Little, Brown, 1968).
15. See Robert L. Bish and Vincent Ostrom, Understanding Urban Government (Washington, D.C., American Enterprise Institute for Public Policy Research, 1974).
16. Allman, "The Urban Crisis Leaves Town," p. 47.
17. Jerome Zukosky, "What's the Problem?" National Civic Review 59 (September 1970).
18. John N. Kolesar, "The States and Urban Planning and Development," in The States and the Urban Crisis, ed. Alan K. Campbell (Englewood Cliffs, N.J.: Prentice-Hall, 1970), pp. 114-38.
19. See the essays in Campbell, The States and the Urban Crisis, for discussions on inadequate state assistance to urban areas.
20. William G. Colman, Cities, Suburbs, and States (New York: Free Press, 1975), p. 257.

21. Charles Press and Charles R. Adrian, "Why Our State Governments Are Sick," Antioch Review 24, no. 2 (1964):149-65.
22. Ira Sharkansky, The Maligned States (New York: McGraw-Hill, 1972).
23. Ibid, p. 150.
24. Paul N. Ylvisaker, "The Growing Role of State Government in Local Affairs," State Government, Summer 1968, pp. 150-156.
25. Norman Beckman and Page L. Ingraham, "The States and Urban Areas," Law and Contemporary Problems 30 (Winter 1965):76-102.
26. Daniel J. Elazar, "The New Federalism: Can the States be Trusted?" The Public Interest, no. 35 (Spring 1974):89-102.
27. Ibid.
28. Jeanne Walker and David Walker, "Rationalizing Local Government Powers, Functions and Structures," State Responsibilities to Local Governments: An Action Agenda, National Governor's Conference, Washington, D.C., October 1975, pp. 38-54.
29. Ibid.
30. Harvey C. Mansfield, "Functions of State and Local Government," in The Fifty States and Their Local Governments, ed. James W. Fesler et al. (New York: Knopf, 1967), p. 116.
31. Allan Rosenbaum, Federal Programs and State Governments: On Understanding Why 40 Years of Federal Efforts Haven't Fundamentally Altered Economic Inequity in American Society, paper delivered at the 1978 Annual Meeting of the American Political Science Association, New York, August 31-September 3, 1978.
32. Ibid., p. 9.
33. Ibid., pp. 10-15.

Chapter 2

METROPOLITANIZATION

INTRODUCTION

Metropolises arise when cities, suburbs, outlying villages, and like communities grow together and become increasingly interdependent. Further, metropolitanization is a process whereby populations and economic activities decentralize among subunits of urban areas. It is this process which we feel is at the heart of growth and decline in different urban areas. The effect of metropolitanization is a "sorting out" and greater interdependence of population and economic activities between cities and suburbs, and among suburbs themselves. The process is much more advanced in larger areas like the New York and Los Angeles metropolitan areas than it is in smaller urban areas such as Athens, Georgia and Rockville, Maryland. Nevertheless, the process is occurring throughout the country and has common features despite regional or geographical differences among urban areas. We contend that what is of most significance is not so much how large or crowded urban areas are, but rather the process of metropolitanization which contributes to many of our urban problems while providing many of the benefits of metropolitan life.

    The process of metropolitanization is reinforced by a system of multiple decentralized local governments which have policy authority over subareas of the metropolis. There are no metropolitanwide governments with policymaking authority which fully encompass metropolitanization as it occurs in the United States. It is the states which have the widest range of powers to respond to metropolitanization. States, if they choose, can alter local service delivery, change financing arrangements and formulas, adjust local government boundaries, and grant or withhold local government home rule in light of metropolitanization. Metropolitanization is reinforced by decentralized local governmental systems which do not give metropolitan areas a single sense of community. These are the themes we pursue in this chapter in order to see the potential role of the states.

All urban areas in the United States are being subjected and are responding to this single process of growth, metropolitanization, whether they be as large as Los Angeles, California or as small as Las Cruces, New Mexico. No urban areas are immune to metropolitanization. They are just at different points of a single continuum. Some regions of the country, such as the South, are now experiencing the effects of metropolitanization which have been evident in the Northeast for decades. Compounding the effects of this process is the above-mentioned fact that no such metropolitanizing area has a single local government which encompasses the entire process. Metropolitanization spills over local governments in urban areas and in fact spills into nonmetropolitan areas. Let us turn to a discussion of metropolitanization and its effects.

AN ORGANIZATION OF SPACE

Metropolitanization is a process whereby urban space is organized to perform various functions. Urban space is organized with strikingly similar patterns from one urban area to another. Residences are separated geographically from industry; high-income residential areas are separate from areas where the poor reside; and minority groups usually live in areas separate from the white middle class. The organization of space into subareas of specific functions and characteristics is increasing. The complexity of the utilization of space is the hallmark of the process of metropolitanization. Before turning to a detailed description of the process and a discussion of its consequences, we would like to define metropolitan areas in territorial terms.

Defining Metropolitan Areas

The term "metropolis," originally applying to Greek city-states such as Athens and Sparta, came to be used to describe any large urban area such as London or New York. More recently in the United States, "metropolitan" has taken on a specific definition and is referred to as a Standard Metropolitan Statistical Area (SMSA), the definition we will use in our discussion. Although there are several definitions of metropolitan areas, the SMSA is the most commonly used. SMSAs are defined and designated by the Office of Federal Statistical Policy and Standards of the U.S. Department of Commerce.[1] The term has gone through several changes in definition since it was first used by the

Census Bureau. Currently, as SMSA is defined as an entire county with a central city of at least 50,000 population or reasonable equivalents of a 50,000 population such as two adjoining cities which have a total population of 50,000. Any contiguous county is also included in the SMSA if 75% of its labor force are in nonagricultural occupations and if 30% work in the central SMSA county. If these conditions are not met, other criteria involving work and commuting patterns can be used to determine which adjacent counties are to be included with the central county in an SMSA. Because most governmental data on urban areas are gathered in accordance with the SMSA definitions, this common definition allows for systematic gathering of information and comparative analysis of all metropolitan areas.

The designation SMSA is a dynamic definition based upon criteria used to encompass areas which demonstrate metropolitan characteristics. That is, as urban areas grow and fringe areas are tied to the center by economic and commuting linkages, they are included in the SMSA. Thus the number of counties included in an SMSA can grow. For example, the Atlanta SMSA grew from five to seven counties between 1960 and 1970 owing to the fact that two additional counties came to meet SMSA criteria. The Washington, D.C. SMSA added Maryland's Charles County in order to reflect the growing urbanization of the county and the number of its residents who are nonagricultural labor and who commute to Washington to work. But there are also counties that exaggerate the true extent of metropolitanization. Pima County--the Tucson, Arizona SMSA--extends over 9000 square miles, as much as Connecticut and Rhode Island combined, but the actual Tucson metropolis proper only occupies a very small portion of that area.

The changes in definition have been the result of an attempt to keep up with the metropolitan process. The current SMSA definition approximates the process in that it includes some areas that are not entirely urban. In addition to sociological and economic reasons, there have also been political motivations for changing the criteria which define the SMSA. To some extent, certain changes in definition have been the result of pressures from localities and citizens who are anxious to gain the appellation "metropolitan area" as a sign of progress, advancement, and the connotation of being cosmopolitan that comes with a metropolitan identification. An additional motivation is that metropolitan areas qualify for some federal aid which nonmetropolitan areas are not eligible to receive. Politically, localities can achieve a SMSA designation by annexing population to the central city to meet the 50,000 minimum.

A National Trend

Metropolitanization is occurring throughout the entire nation, but at varying rates within the different regions. Approximately 70% of the U.S. population lives in metropolitan areas. As Table 2.1 indicates, the proportion of the total United States population living in metropolitan areas increased from 62 to 68.6% between 1950 and 1974. Regionally, the metropolitan areas in the West and South are growing at a faster rate than those in the Northeast and the North Central regions. Metropolitan growth, which was first evidenced in the Northeast and the North Central areas, has now taken hold in the rest of the country.

The process of metropolitanization now appears to be in an advanced stage in that growth in metropolitan areas is spilling over into adjacent nonmetropolitan areas. That is, those areas not classified as metropolitan, but that adjoin metropolitan areas, are growing. The growth in nonmetropolitan areas is not a return to rural life, but a consequence of creating metropolitan patterns on a wider scale. The pattern rests upon a relationship of the city to the suburban fringe which utilizes territory to perform increasingly specialized functions. Eventually, as contiguous nonmetropolitan areas become socially and economically integrated with metropolitan areas, they will be redefined as metropolitan. Or if the nonmetropolitan areas gain sufficient population in their own right, they will, according to the classification scheme of the federal Office of Management and the Budget, also become SMSAs.

Table 2.1 also shows how, in 1970, population within metropolitan areas was divided between central city, suburban areas, and nonmetropolitan areas respectively at 31.5, 37.1, and 31.4%. Although the total metropolitan populations have been growing, the increase has actually been exclusively in suburban growth. Suburban areas have been continuously increasing in population over the last several decades, whereas central cities generally have been losing population. Where central cities have grown, such as in the West, it has been a result of annexation rather than natural increases. If fast-growing central cities such as Houston and Phoenix did not annex suburban areas, they would have lost population based upon their old city limits.

The president's national urban policy indicates that today's widespread population loss in the nation's central cities is unprecedented.[2] While some central cities have lost population for many years, most cities have not done so until recently. In the early 1970s alone, 7 million more people moved out of the central cities than moved in. Table 2.2 indicates that for the central cities in large SMSAs, loss of jobs

20 / Metropolitanization

Table 2.1 Change in Population of Metropolitan and Nonmetropolitan Areas, by Region, 1950-1960, 1960-1970, 1970-1974 (thousands)

	1950[a]	1960[a]	1970[a]	Percentage change, 1950-1960	Percentage change 1960-1970	1970[b]	1974[b]	Percentage change, 1970-1974[c]
United States, total	151,326	179,323	203,300	+18.50	+13.37	199,819	207,949	+10.17
All metropolitan areas								
Total	94,579	119,595	139,419	+26.45	+16.58	137,058	142,043	+ 9.09
In central cities	53,696	59,947	63,797	+11.64	+ 6.42	62,876	61,650	- 4.87
Outside central cities	40,883	59,648	75,622	+45.90	+26.78	74,182	80,394	+20.93
Nonmetropolitan areas								
Total	56,747	59,728	63,831	+ 5.25	+ 6.95	62,761	65,905	+12.52
Northeast, total	39,478	44,678	49,061	+13.17	+ 9.81	48,329	48,887	+ 2.89
All metropolitan areas								
Total	31,687	35,878	39,007	+13.23	+ 8.72	38,675	38,742	+ 0.43
In central cities	18,017	17,498	17,167	- 2.88	- 1.89	17,044	16,250	-11.65
Outside central cities	13,670	18,380	21,840	+34.46	+18.82	21,631	22,493	+ 9.96
Nonmetropolitan areas								
Total	7,791	8,800	10,054	+12.95	+14.25	9,655	10,145	+12.69
North Central, total	44,461	51,619	56,591	+16.10	+ 9.63	55,793	56,522	+ 3.27
All metropolitan areas								
Total	27,090	33,536	37,867	+23.79	+12.91	37,173	37,562	+ 2.62
In central cities	16,269	17,036	17,184	+ 4.71	+ 0.87	16,861	15,941	-13.64
Outside central cities	10,821	16,500	20,083	+52.48	+25.35	20,312	21,621	+16.11
Nonmetropolitan areas								
Total	17,371	18,083	18,724	+ 4.10	+ 3.54	18,620	18,960	+ 4.56

An Organization of Space / 21

South, total	47,197	54,973	62,812	+16.48	+14.26	61,603	65,703	+16.64
All metropolitan areas								
Total	21,410	28,853	35,173	+34.76	+21.90	34,416	37,046	+19.10
In central cities	12,162	15,619	17,890	+28.42	+14.54	17,609	17,592	− 0.24
Outside central cities	9,248	13,234	17,283	+43.10	+30.60	16,807	19,454	+39.37
Nonmetropolitan areas								
Total	25,787	26,120	27,639	+ 1.29	+ 5.82	27,187	28,657	+13.52
West, total	20,190	28,053	34,836	+38.95	+24.18	34,094	36,837	+20.11
All metropolitan areas								
Total	14,391	21,328	27,373	+48.20	+28.34	26,795	28,693	+21.11
In central cities	7,247	9,794	11,555	+35.15	+17.98	11,362	11,867	+11.11
Outside central cities	7,144	11,534	15,818	+61.45	+37.14	15,433	16,826	+22.57
Nonmetropolitan areas								
Total	5,799	6,725	7,463	+15.97	+10.97	7,299	8,144	+28.94

Percentage Distribution

Metropolitan	62.57	66.4	68.6
Central city	35.50	33.3	31.5
Suburban	27.0	35.1	37.1
Nonmetropolitan	37.5	36.6	31.4

[a] Figures relate to areas as defined for 1970.
[b] Figures relate to areas as defined for 1974, including later adjustements for 1970.
[c] Rate per decade.

Sources: U.S. Department of Commerce, Bureau of the Census, "Estimates of Population of [state name]: Counties and Metropolitan Areas," Current Population Reports, Series P-26, nos. 75-1 to 75-50 (Washington, D.C.: U.S. Government Printing Office, July 1974 and 1975); and Censuses of Population for 1950, 1960, and 1970, as seen in CED, 1977.

Table 2.2 Change in Central-city Jobs and Population for Ten Large SMSAs, 1960-1970

SMSA	Percentage change in jobs	Percentage change in population
New York	- 1.9	+ 1.4
Chicago	-12.1	- 5.1
Philadelphia	- 4.1	- 2.6
Detroit	-18.8	- 9.4
Boston	-14.2	- 8.0
St. Louis	-14.2	-17.0
Baltimore	- 4.6	- 3.5
Cleveland	-12.9	-14.2
Newark	-12.5	- 5.6
Milwaukee	-10.2	- 3.2

Source: The President's Urban and Regional Policy Group Report, A New Partnership to Conserve America's Communities (March 1978), pp. 1-18.

has been greater than loss of population, but there has been an exodus of both jobs and people to the suburbs. Central cities are declining not only as places to live but also as places of employment, in either absolute terms or relative to suburban areas. As critical as the population and job loss in central cities has been as such, it is also important to note who is leaving. Generally, the people who are leaving central cities tend to be richer, better educated, less often of minority status, and younger than those who are staying behind.

Interdependencies, Specialization, and Decentralization

The term "metropolis," as used by social scientists today, covers more than the self-contained city-state community originally meant by it, and it covers a far wider range of settlements. Metropolitan areas in the United States today vary in population from only 50,000 in Las Cruces, New Mexico to over 10,000,000 in the New York area. While such size and density are important, they are not sufficient for understanding metropolitan areas. In the sense used by urban researchers, "metropolitan" describes a substantially greater complex which includes several characteristics: interdependence, specialization, and decentralization.

An Organization of Space / 23

The specific subareas of the metropolis are generally not self-contained little cities alone, but rather they are areas specialized according to function and characteristics of the population. Many functions and activities are specific to a location in the modern metropolis: certain areas may be exclusively residential, other areas may be predominantly industrial. Subareas may be entertainment districts or commercial centers. Urban populations usually do not live and work in the same subarea of the metropolis. In fact, metropolitanization has come to mean not only the separation of residence from work, but the separation of basic types of life-style activities from one another. The separation of functions in metropolitan areas is much more complex than the city-suburb difference often cited.

The process of metropolitanization is altering the basic relationship between core (central city) and fringe (suburbia). Central cities are increasingly left to the poor, minorities, the elderly, single adults, and childless couples. The basic functions of the "city," such as a center for employment, cultural activities, entertainment, and wholesale and retail activities are no longer exclusively the domain of central cities. Increasingly these functions and activities can be found in specialized areas throughout the entire metropolitan area. There are "downtowns" in many sectors of the modern metropolis. With the exception of a few activities, such as those requiring continuous face-to-face contact, most functions can be performed in any sector of the metropolis as long as transportation and communication networks exist. The highway system and the telecommunication systems have allowed erstwhile "central-city" functions to spread to the entire metropolitan area.

Likewise, suburbs are not exclusively residential communities. There are suburban areas that are based principally upon industrial or commercial activities. The ubiquitous suburban shopping malls attest to the fact that residents do not have to go downtown to meet their basic consumption needs. Examinations of commuting patterns indicates that ever-increasing proportions of individuals travel within and between suburban areas rather than commuting from suburb to city and back. Moreover, there is a great deal of variance among suburban areas as to the characteristics of their residents. There are suburban enclosures of the very wealthy, the middle-income, and the poor. Rarely are these different income groups found integrated in the same suburban locality. The individual suburban localities are quite homogeneous as to the characteristics of their populations and their basic economic activities. Country clubs are not likely to be found mixed among steel mills and automobile assembly plants. Suburbs, when viewed singly, are often seen as quite homogeneous; however, when the entire suburban area is examined it is found to be quite heterogeneous, composed of many and varied subareas.

Historically, urban areas have consisted of densely populated centers with the population density decreasing as one moved further out to the fringes. Until the last part of the nineteenth century, most cities were geographically small, densely populated, and largely self-contained. This description has become increasingly less accurate as metropolitanization has proceeded. In that sense, owing to those advances in transportation and communications, metropolitanization has been tantamount to "urban sprawl," as people have been able to move out and to settle in less dense patterns. The population growth in our metropolitan areas has therefore actually been accompanied by a fall in densities. In the twenty years prior to 1970, when urbanized land nearly tripled, average density fell from 8.4 persons per acre in 1950 to 5.3 in 1970. Central city densities fell from 12 persons per acre in 1950 to 7 in 1970.[3] The population densities of entire metropolitan areas, both central cities and suburbs, are several times smaller than were the densities of cities at the start of the twentieth century. If the boundaries remain the same, the decrease in population means a less dense population settlement. New York, Chicago, Philadelphia--all large central cities--are less densely populated than they were several decades ago.[4] But metropolitan theory predicts that in older metropolitan areas density will decline less and less rapidly; "urban sprawl" is not expected to continue much beyond current SMSA boundaries as population growth more and more fills in the suburbs and surrounding counties already within those areas. That is, in fact, what has begun to happen, as shown in Table 2.3. In urban areas during 1950-1960 the density rate decline was 31%; during 1960-1970, the density declined at the much lower rate of 10%.

The basic economics of urban development in the United States indicates that it is less expensive to build on vacant fringe land than it is to rebuild upon land in the center. Whether the energy crisis will influence the development pattern to make it more compact and dense remains to be seen. However, the basic forces of "spread" development are solidly entrenched. The highway system is in place and facilitates a low-density development pattern. In addition, many of the activities that were formerly anchored to downtown are now themselves spread over the metropolis. There is less reason at this state of the metropolitan process to reconcentrate population and economic activities in a centralized location.

Metropolitan areas are highly interdependent systems. Very few subareas are self-contained. They are specialized. The individuals of high-income areas must travel to their businesses or professional offices. The domestic workers and yard maintenance employees of the

Table 2.3 Densities of Central Cities, Urbanized Areas, and Urbanized Area Noncentral Cities, 1950, 1960, and 1970

Density (persons per square mile)		Percentage rate of decline
All urbanized areas		
1950	5408	
1960	3752	31
1970	3376	10
Central cities		
1950	7786	
1960	Not given	
1970	4463	40
Noncentral cities in urban areas		
1950	3167	
1960	Not given	
1970	2627	17

Source: Based on data in Advisory Commission on Inter-governmental Relations, Improving Urban America: A Challenge to Federalism (Washington, D.C.: U.S. Government Printing Office, 1976), p. 211.

high-income residents cannot afford to live in such areas. In essence, if there is to be a high-income residential area, there must also be an industrial area, a commercial area, and a low-income area. Specialized areas could not be initiated or exist independently of other areas. The sum total of all the specialized subareas thus makes for a highly interdependent total metropolis.

It is this combination of specialized areas, decentralized patterns of development, and interdependence that is the definition of metropolitanization. This complex urban system is rarely grasped by reliance on demographic descriptions of size and density alone. Yet this metropolitan pattern is basically a singular pattern repeated in each of our urban areas. There are no urban areas which are growing contrary to these basic processes. Where deviations exist, they are minor and are adaptations of metropolitanization to geographical or territorial constraints. Deviations are only variations on a metropolitanization theme.

Changing Demands and Metropolitanization

Urbanization and metropolitanization bring with them a growing necessity for public institutions to meet public needs, and as population grows so does the number of needs that can only be met by such public, governmental institutions. Today such matters as medical and consumer information, housing and employment, education and retirement, safety and sanitation, (not to mention such traditional governmental matters as defense) are all the concern of public institutions. And we understandably expect these institutions of ours to be efficient and innovative, honest and responsive, and consciously concerned with such factors as our safety, our environment, our nutrition, and the like. As our society has grown, the list of these needs and expectations has grown vastly from our frontier days.

Since that time, our demands have changed with advances in technology which have resulted in commensurate advances in our population's economic situation and standard of living. Thus today there are more goods and services available to more people in this country than ever before, and we accordingly have higher expectations of comfort and convenience than did the frontier family which had to carve out a road, build a house, and provide fire, water, and other "services" for itself.

Thus our metropolises evolved out of the changed demands and means to fulfill them resulting from those technological advances. And the character of the metropolitan area reflects the way that space has been used to achieve the values implicit in those demands. When the metropolis no longer satisfies its residents' aspirations, just as when the residents of rural areas no longer find satisfaction there, they move on. This movement from city to suburbanized metropolitan area, to a multinucleated metropolitan area, in order to fulfill individual values, is reflected in population shifts and life-style differences. Americans are leaving their central cities and show no real interest in renewing them, because we have open areas and easy access to them, which makes moving and building anew more economic than staying and rebuilding; hence decentralization.

Possession of a standard yardstick, the Standard Metropolitan Statistical Area measure, has enabled researchers to plot changes in metropolitan areas as these areas have aged. The changes are profuse: increased population and developed land area, decreased population densities for the area, increased numbers of suburban communities, and reduced distinctions between central cities and many suburban communities. These city-suburb distinctions are apparent in standard of living, in quality of life, in rates of commercial-industrial-residential development, and in residents' characteristics, as seen in Table 2.4.

Table 2.4 Metropolitan Area Families with Incomes over $15,000 and under $5,000, 1971

	Percentage of families		Ratio of well-to-do to poor
	Over $15,000	Under $5,000	
White			
Central city	26.7	15.7	1.701
Outside central city	33.2	11.3	2.938
Black			
Central city	11.3	35.6	0.317
Outside central city	16.9	28.0	0.604

Source: Statistical Abstract of the United States, 1974 (Washington, D.C.: U.S. Government Printing Office, 1973), p. 331.

Apart from this central city-suburb differentiation, there is that between suburbs themselves. Yet while suburbs show diversity, they are more alike than they are like the central city. In their recent study on suburbs, Murphy and Rehfuss found that while suburbs are not necessarily homogeneous, some actually may have more "central-city" than "suburban" characteristics because of the nature of their population.[5] It can be argued that the smaller-sized central cities of smaller metropolitan areas hold no more attractions than suburban communities in the much larger and older metropolitan areas of our country.[6] The distinction between a central city and a suburban city in some areas has become a definition in name only.

The decline in business property and retail activities means that revenue to government will decrease, causing still more extensive fiscal disparities in metropolitan areas. Now that immigration to the cities has slowed, intrasuburban movement is the most common redistribution pattern. As expected in this current stage of metropolitan area life, where intrasuburban movement is more common than mass exodus to nonmetropolitan areas, the nonmetropolitan area growth remained at an almost constant rate of 5.2% for the 1950s, 6.95% for the 1960s, but climbed to 12.57% for 1970-1974, as shown in Table 2.1. In the areas that have been metropolitan the longest, the suburban residents have become increasingly self-sufficient, no longer needing substantial contact with the central city.

The metropolitan area process can be described as postcity America. This process includes the shift of the economic center of gravity from cities to suburban rings of metropolitan areas; the increasing concentration and isolation of the poor, the elderly, and disadvantaged minority groups in central cities; and the continuing relative deterioration of the economic condition of central cities.

As Willbern notes, the basic purpose of the city is the facilitation of interchange.[7] Because the means of interchange have altered (e.g., we have better transportation and communication), the nature of the city has latered (e.g., it spreads out as there is no longer any need for physically centralized interchange). One could argue that people would still prefer the centralized interchange of goods, services, and information of the pre-1940s, but that the technological changes have facilitated decentralization interchange. That is true for all population segments except the poor. To take advantage of the ease of decentralized interchange through technology in fact does cost money. Thus the poor stay in the city, where the cheaper centralized interchange still exists, and until decentralized interchange is as inexpensive as centralized interchange, as exemplified in the science fiction future of teleportation, the poor will remain concentrated in the cities. In this relative sense, decentralized interchange is more expensive for the average citizen than centralized interchange. But it is less expensive for the entrepreneurs who control development. Manufacturing's need for space forced companies to move outward just as people did, which also promoted decentralization. Clearly one could again argue that if centralization of interchange were somehow the path of least resistance, rather than decentralization of interchange, people would still be in the cities, as would manufacturing.

GOVERNMENTAL DECENTRALIZATION IN THE METROPOLIS

The social and economic diversification within metropolitan areas is reinforced by a decentralized local governmental system. None of the nation's metropolitan areas has a single, autonomous, centralized local government. There is no metropolitanwide government in the United States. Even consolidated governments such as Jacksonville-Duval County, Florida and Nashville-Davidson County, Tennessee have a multiplicity of local governments within their boundaries. Local government decentralization to a greater or lesser degree is a given for metropolitan areas. Moreover, the local governments in the metropolitan area have political autonomy independent of one another. Many local jurisdictions make decisions in the metropolis that affect its character and the direction of its growth. Before discussing the implication of a decentralized local government system, let us look at the number and types of jurisdictions.

Table 2.5 indicates that there are approximately 25,000 local governments in the nation's 272 SMSAs. This represents an average of about 200 local governments per metropolitan area. Although the number of SMSAs has increased from 264 in 1972 to 272 in 1977, a 3% increase, the rate of increase of local governments has been greater. The increase in the five-year period has been 16.7% from 22,185 to 25,896. The multiplicity has not only been sustained but has increased its pace.

As shown in Table 2.6, the highest number of local governments in large metropolitan areas ranges from approximately 1200 for Chicago down to 362 for New York. Although there is some direct relationship between the size of population of an SMSA and the total number of governments, the smaller SMSAs have more local jurisdictions per capita. Thus, while governmental decentralization is a characteristic of all metropolitan areas, it does not increase with increases of SMSA size.

The decentralized governmental pattern further indicates that many residents of SMSAs live in relatively small political jurisdictions. In 1970, approximately 38% of SMSA residents lived in local jurisdictions with populations of 25,000 or less. Metropolitan areas are governered to a large extent by small jurisdictions. There is a continuing increase in the number and percentage of people living in local governments of 50,000 or less. When the populations of these small governmental units are examined, we see what this implies: although metro-

Table 2.5 Number of Local Governments in Metropolitan Areas, 1957-1977

	1977	1972	1967	1962	1957
SMSAs	272	264	227	212	174
Counties	594	444	404	310	266
Municipalities	6,444	5,467	4,977	4,142	3,422
Townships	4,031	3,462	3,255	2,575	2,317
School districts	5,220	4,758	5,018	6,004	6,473
Other special districts	9,580	8,054	7,040	5,411	3,180
Totals	25,869	22,185	20,703	18,442	15,658

Source: Based on data in the 1972 and 1977 editions of Bureau of the Census, U.S. Department of Commerce, Governmental Organization, vol. 1, no. 1, Census of Governments (Washington, D.C.: U.S. Government Printing Office, 1978), pp. 12-14.

Table 2.6 Ten SMSAs with Largest Number of Governments, 1977

Chicago	1172
Philadelphia	852
Pittsburgh	698
New York	538
St. Louis	483
Houston	304
San Francisco-Oakland	302
Portland	298
Indianapolis	296
Denver	272

Source: Bureau of the Census, U.S. Department of Commerce, Census of Governments, 1977 (Washington, D.C.: U.S. Government Printing Office, July 1978).

politanization has increased the diversity of subpopulations within SMSAs as described above, many of the smaller local jurisdictions within SMSAs have homogeneous populations. Many jurisdictions are composed only of the wealthy, the middle class, or high-value industrial property. Thus the social and economic mosaic of SMSAs is reinforced by local governmental authority. Local governmental authority includes the ability to raise local taxes, the most important of which is the property tax. The ability to raise taxes is related to the type and quality of services a community can provide. Some jurisdictions may be wealthy, segregated enclaves, while neighboring jurisdictions may be populated with minorities and have little taxable resources.

Multiple local governments in a compacted area create difficulties in dealing with the problems involved not only in taxation, but also in transportation, education, poverty, race, health, housing, crime, pollution, recreation, and sanitation. Problems in these areas often stimulate great demands on local governments to provide new or more sophisticated levels of services. At the same time, however, many of these governments are small, part-time operations administered by nonprofessionals. The decentralized nature of local governments in these metropolitan areas limits the revenue available to many local governments with which to attack the problems. This happens because some jurisdictions have needs that go beyond their resources even with high taxes, while other jurisdictions have a greater tax base and are able to keep their taxes low. The resulting negative externalities, such as increased traffic in one jurisdiction as a result of shopping center activities in a neighboring government, and inequalities are recognized and become the focus of public dissatisfaction. People tend to blame local and state governments for their problems because they are the governments most directly involved in service delivery.

The issue of educational financing in metropolitan areas provides an example of both the problems involved and the proposed solutions. As indicated above, in most metropolitan areas there is an increasing separation of place of work from residence. This separation has meant an increasing homogeneity within an area serviced by a school district; thus there may be increasing disparities when compared with other districts which, in turn, leads to disparities in levels of per-pupil property valuation assessments. More often than not, the disparity focuses on central cities versus suburban schools. Many people claim the fiscal disparities then translate into quality-of-education disparities.

The differences in assessments can be startling; for instance, one New Jersey community had a per-pupil assessment of $5.5 million, while a neighboring district had a per-pupil assessment of only $33,000.[8] A well-known case is that of Serrano v. Priest, of 1971. The California community of Beverly Hills had a property value of $200,000 per pupil and spent $1244 on each public school student for education. Neighboring Baldwin Park had a property tax rate which was twice that of Beverly Hills yet was able to raise less than $500 per child. This type of inequality has meant that poorer jurisdictions have often looked to the states to provide equal educational opportunity through equalizing financial arrangements while wealthier districts frequently oppose the equalization formulas that states have proposed since they have to pay for it.

THE NATURE OF COMMUNITY IN METROPOLITAN AREAS

Arguments for reorganization of governance in metropolitan areas range from demands for neighborhood arrangements to calls for some form of areawide or regional control. Behind such arguments rests a vision of community; but what is the nature of that vision? A community can be a physical concentration of individuals in one place, or it can be a social organization among persons who may or may not reside in an identifiable geographic area.

When people live in the same place, community develops because living together in an area gives people common perspectives and encourages them to work together in an organized fashion. From another perspective, community is also a mental attitude that arises from feelings of interdependence and loyalty. Change destroyed the oldest form of physical community--the agricultural village where people had a shared fate, lived isolated from other communities, and were involved in intense interactions, interdependencies, and communication.[9] Because of mass communications, mass educational networks, and functional specializations, new styles and types of community are being developed today. If a person belongs to more than one type of community organization, he or she will have numerous loyalties. Local political activity creates a sense of community because it provides services, social controls, and identity.

Has the notion of the community as a defined geographic area with specific boundaries become less viable with the proliferation of overlapping local governments? This may very well be so in metropolitan areas where the overlapping and division of functions is extreme and citizen familiarity with community affairs and political responsibility relatively low. The local community has become increasingly bound to the larger society, and in this process, various parts of the community--such as the educational system, recreation, economic units, etc.--have become increasingly oriented toward areawide, state, or national concerns and less oriented toward each other.[10] As localities have been more integrated in metropolitan, state, and national systems, many of the essential decisions about their structure and services have been preempted, leaving less scope of action for the local community. The community relationships with other units in the state and national systems are seen as a vertical pattern of relationships. In past years, community relations have in actuality been more often horizontal because the actions were guided by local associations and systematized through a common network.

In this country, communities are essentially political, founded by people with immediate common interests rather than organic or familial ties.[11] The basis for such a community and community institutions is the maintenance of common political goals. Such communities are identified as "civil communities" in contrast with organic communities or agricultural village types where the same families reside in the same place over many generations.[12] Not every community with its own local government is a civil community. If the entity is very small, the community may be capable of political expression but not capable of self-government. If the entity is large, it probably will be made up of sets of subcommunities that have few if any common civic goals of a local character and may even have conflicting local interest. The existence of a civil community depends more on its internal workings and the type of existing political communication than it does on political boundaries. Studies done by the Advisory Commission on Intergovernmental Relations (ACIR) indicate that in cities over 250,000 the size of the population becomes dysfunctional and intensifies urban problems, while in cities under 24,000, services cannot be provided efficiently and comprehensively.[13] In cities in the 25,000-250,000 range, size matters less, and neither economies or diseconomies of scale are significant.

The metropolis can be referred to as a community only in the most generalized economic sense. It is a community only in that residents will say they are from Chicago, New York, or some other metropolitan area. In essence, the metropolis is made up of many communities. These communities are more often than not functional communities based upon shared interests that have no clear geographic boundary. To the extent that geographically based political communities exist they are much less extensive in scope than metropolitan areas. Political communities may be based upon a neighborhood association united to protect property rights, or communities may be evidenced in the sense that Elazar identifies as a civil community. Civil communities have limited purposes and pursue a few objectives such as personal security and educational values. Viewing the metropolis as a single political community has been the misconception upon which numerous reforms calling for areawide government have foundered.

STATES AND METROPOLITAN AREAS: AN OVERVIEW

The federal system is built on the concept of multiple polities. The system was established with the intention that national, state, and local governments would interact through cooperation and conflict to balance out each other's power. This system now has to work within the context of metropolitanization, and metropolitanization has affected all three levels of governments and their relationships. The problems and strains on local government that accompany metropolitanization have insured the involvement of the national government in matters that were once purely state-local. The national government has provided financial assistance, but the involvement is necessarily limited constitutionally and practically. For the present, the two governments most involved in dealing with the problems of metropolitanization are the states and urban local governments.

Metropolitanization has meant that urban areas now contain several legal jurisdictions bordering on each other. The externalities and spillovers that naturally occur have developed into major problems. These problems are changing some assumptions about what should define a local government or community. Local governments have reacted to the problems caused by metropolitanization primarily by asking for financial aid. Some localities have tried to reorganize or modernize their structures, but most local governments have resisted, rejected, or not attempted major structural changes. Since local governments have not been able to resolve their problems, they have looked to the states. States are often portrayed as having the ability, but lacking the desire, to solve metropolitan problems. Supporters and critics of states argue whether the inactivity of states results from real constraints or basic policy.

Over the past ten years, various recommendations have been given to the national, state, and local governments on how to cope with the problems of metropolitanization. Some of these recommendations have been acted upon, but overall no one government has done an adequate job. The problems involved will probably not fade away naturally; rather, it is predicted that they will intensify and provoke crises similar to New York City's financial dilemma. The question as to which government will determine the fate of metropolitan areas is still unanswered.

Downs, in discussing the many hypothetical future patterns possible for metropolitan areas, concludes with this observation:

> State governments are the best focal point for development of any overall strategies controlling future urban growth. They are the only institutions that combine metropolitan perspective, decision powers to override local governments, and sufficient knowledge and local political roots to make use of such powers acceptable.[14]

This is not meant to imply that states should enter the business of governing their metropolitan areas, only that they should not bar the efforts of localities to govern themselves. States cannot by themselves solve metropolitan problems, but they can facilitate local government efforts through technical assistance or development of model standards, through financial assistance, through assumption of certain activities heretofore under local responsibility, or through empowering localities with greater authority.

The 1974 Report on National Growth and Development urged such a state role:

> The states are particularly well-suited to guiding and managing growth because of their special place in our federal system. The states combine metropolitan perspectives, decisive powers to influence local community actions which affect larger interests, and sufficient knowledge and local political roots to make effective use of these too. The states can tax, regulate and invest in ways that will induce new industry to develop in particular areas and to influence

where land development and economic growth may take place within a state.[15]

States and localities are being asked to assume leadership in solving their own problems. The next chapter explores the roles of these two polities, how they have responded in the past to the problems caused by metropolitanization, and what they are being asked to do now.

NOTES

1. For a description of the criteria used in defining SMSAs, see U.S. Office of Management and the Budget, Criteria Followed in Establishing Standard Metropolitan Statistical Areas, rev. ed. (Washington, D.C.: U.S. Government Printing Office, 1975).
2. The President's Urban and Regional Policy Group Report, A New Partnership to Conserve America's Communities (Washington, D.C., March 1978), pp. 1-9.
3. U.S. Domestic Council, Committee on County Development, Department of HUD, Report on National Growth and Development (1972), p. 29.
4. York Willbern, The Withering Away of the City (Bloomington: Indiana University Press, 1967), p. 25.
5. Thomas P. Murphy and John Rehfuss, Urban Politics in the Suburbs (Homewood, Ill.: Dorsey Press, 1976), p. 17.
6. James W. Hughes, "Dilemmas of Suburbanization and Growth Controls," Annals of American Academy of Political and Social Sciences 422 (November 1975):61-76.
7. Willbern, "The Withering Away of the City," p. 14.
8. Robert Wood, 1400 Governments: The Political Economy of the Metropolitan Region (Cambridge: Harvard University, 1961), p. 55.
9. David Minar and Scott Greer, The Concept of Community (Chicago: Aldine, 1969), pp. x-xi.
10. Roland Warren, The Community in America (Chicago: Rand McNally, 1963), p. 5.
11. Daniel Elazar, "State-Local Relations: Revising Old Theories for New Practics," paper prepared for Fourth Annual Town Conference, October 1975, p. 60.
12. Ibid., p. 61.
13. Advisory Commission on Intergovernmental Relations, Regionalism Revisited: Recent Articles and Local Responses (Washington, D.C.: U.S. Government Printing Office, 1977).

14. Anthony Downs, "Alternative Forms of Future Urban Growth in the U.S.," in The Uneasy Partnership: The Dynamics of Federal, State, and Urban Relations, ed. Richard D. Feld (Palo Alto, Calif.: National Press Books, 1973), p. 178.
15. U.S. Domestic Council, Report on National Growth and Development, p. 143.

Chapter 3

THE STATES, FEDERALISM, AND HOME RULE

INTRODUCTION

We have discussed how local governments are confronted with increasing and diversifying demands as the process of metropolitanization continues. We have further commented upon the changing nature of community in metropolitan areas. There are increasingly fewer places which are self-contained, where the basic needs of the residents are met within a single local jurisdiction. Governmentally, authority in the United States is divided among many political jurisdictions. Populations, whether they be communities or not, live in a federal system with divided governmental authority. We now turn our attention to the nature of the federal system and discuss how it is being affected by metropolitanization. In our discussion we want to highlight the particular role of the state and the nature of home rule for local governments.

THE WEB OF GOVERNMENT

The federal principle calling for two concurrent levels of governance is ingrained into the American historic fabric. The Constitution explicitly requires that governing power be divided between the national and state governments. Although local governments are not constitutionally included in this federal system, in reality the basic relationship involving shared power has been expanded to include local governments. Thus, for two hundred years our federal system has been characterized by three political spheres, national, state, and local, each seeking to balance interactions with the others.

In the last twenty years a new element, metropolitanization, has become an increasingly important factor in the power juggling. Metropolitanization is affecting federalism by altering the working relationships of all three polities. Local governments must incorporate new and intricate considerations in attempts to respond to the needs and demands of their populations. Decisions that were once relatively clearcut become complicated as their impacts on neighboring communities are recognized. The selection of a landfill site, the development of a new shopping mall, or the building of a hospital in one community can generate positive and negative consequences in some or all of the adjacent communities. Try as they might, localities can no longer prevent spillover effects of many of their decisions. States and the national government necessarily become involved as cities and communities look to them for allies, mediators, or authoritative decision makers. Cooperative and conflicting relationships between polities emerge and disappear, depending on the issue and environment.

The Federal Principle: Two Tiers and Three Sets of Governments

The idea that a people can enter into lasting yet limited political associations for the purpose of reaching common goals and protecting certain rights while still preserving their freedom is the underlying assumption of federalism. In the United States, federalism links the larger government with several smaller ones in such a way as to preserve the internal autonomy of the smaller while establishing a common union. Our federalism is formally characterized by the division of power between the two levels or planes of government, reflecting a noncentralized system wherein the powers of government are distributed among many centers whose existence is guaranteed by the Constitution. Although local governments are not constitutionally included in this federal principle, the basic noncentralized relationship between the national government and states has been extended de facto through the political process to the localities as well.

This noncentralized relationship can be viewed as a matrix of governmental units with power existing in all of them.[1] Governmental power does not flow exclusively from the national government down to local governments. Just as often, the national government acts because state and local governments exert political power to achieve their desires. Thus varied-size governments in a noncentralized system have the capacity to satisfy citizen demands and to survive intact. This noncentralization opens up real possibilities for governmental units of all sizes to maintain the ability to act within the complexities of the whole.

Dual Versus Cooperative Federalism

The Constitution grants governing powers to states and to the national government, defining national ones and reserving the rest for the states, but no local powers were described in the Constitution. This situation, two governments with somewhat separate powers, led to the once-popular concept of dual federalism. Advocates of dual federalism believed that powers could be clearly defined and divided and that, once divided, governments would not need to interfere with each other. The dual federalism concept was also applied to state-local distributions of power. Dual federalism has been characterized as advocacy of a separation of powers so that the national government does not "meddle" in the affairs of the states and the states do not "meddle" in the affairs of localities.[2] In reality, federalism has never been "dual," nor have powers ever been clearly defined or divided, and it is regularly necessary for governments to "meddle" with other governments.

Although the Constitution recognizes two levels of governments and seeks a balance between the two, there is a need for continual judicial interpretation because the division of powers and duties is not rigidly stipulated. Historically, the distribution of powers between the states and the nation has been uncertain. Dual federalism continued for a time during the 1800s to be the predominant legal doctrine, but more recently, particularly after the Great Depression, it came to be viewed as an unrealistic description of governmental and political activities.

Marble Cake, Picket Fence, and Intergovernmental Complexities

Various figurative analogies have been developed to describe the system's workings. Federalism has been called a "layer cake," a "marble cake," a "picket fence," and a "tangled web of rubber bands." These images and others all attempt to portray the cooperation, conflict, chaos, and functionality that the federal system embodies. Cooperation and sharing of functions by polities has been exemplified by the hundreds of national-state-local categorical grants, relief formulas, the General Revenue Sharing of federal funds with states and localities, and the national-local Community Block Grant programs. Conflictive relationships are just as easily identified. Localities and states try to and often do block and frustrate the national government and each other in order to get what they want. At present, local governments often push fiscal burdens onto other units of government while still maintaining "local control" over how the money is to be spent. States and local governments have been fighting over issues such as public school financing through "fiscal equalization" formulas, giving greater assistance to poorer jurisdictions, and the states' desire for the federal government to take over the financing of welfare programs. Wide variations in the philosophies and politics of the fifty states insure a continuing battle over national initiatives in areas such as environmental regulations and health care planning and regulation. From the beginning of the federal republic, cooperation and conflict among federal, state, and local governments existed. Functions are shared among governments, and no function is the exclusive province of one of the levels. Where one level of government is preponderant in a given activity, the other levels are politically influential through money or through intergovernmental relationships. The system is characterized by a chaos of structure, function, and political process where the sharing of functions is in "no neat order."[3]

Chaos may very well be an apt characterization, but this very disorder functions to achieve a multiplicity of goals. For example, this condition of "no neat order" is important to the successful maintenance of state and local autonomy in a highly integrated federal system because the variability of grants-in-aid and other forms of transfer of payments from larger to smaller governments has enabled the smaller governments to maintain their autonomy by choosing from a variety of offers.[4] The system also counteracts the natural tendency of the national government to assume even larger shares of power. Because the authors of the Constitution were very fearful of a single government becoming so powerful that it could usurp the rights of people, they designed the system so that the different governments would limit each other. Some observers say that if local governments were not able to frustrate the federal and state governments, there would be little justification for their existence. Wildavsky and Pressman argue that "if the federal principle maintains its vitality, then it means precisely that state and local organizations must be able to oppose, delay and reject federal initiatives. When these kinds of actions can no longer be undertaken, there is no state or local independence and hence no operative federalism. The form might still be visible but the substance will have disappeared."[5]

The survival of local self-government might be endangered if the system were made more orderly because larger and wealthier governments could then find it easier to control or influence smaller ones. Federalism is thus a functional but open and asymmetrical system; it is simultaneously a battlefield, a coalition, and a recovery plan, and it is beginning to have to deal with the new and potent force of metropolitanization.

INTERDEPENDENCIES OF GOVERNMENTS AND THE SHARING OF POWER

Development of Interdependence

The interdependence within the federal system developed as states found that certain reserved powers became more important when shared with the central government, and the central government found state collaboration helpful in areas wherein it possessed delegated powers.[6] Added to this was the large area of concurrent powers where the state and national governments found it beneficial to collaborate. The joint stock company and the cooperative land survey are two of the major means by which cooperation was achieved in the early 1800s.[7] In practicing cooperative federalism, the factors involved were: a common concern among governments about public programs of wide significance; a way to match resources with needs (for example, at first through land grants and later through money, the central government has been in a position to act as chief instigator and supporter of cooperative federalism); and the setting of national standards while leaving responsibility for administration with states and localities.[8]

Governments sharing functions means one or more of the following conditions of interdependence, according to Grodzins: significant decision making exercised by all planes in the formulation of a program; significant responsibilities in administration of an activity exercised by officials of all governments; and significant influence over the operations of a given program exerted by representatives of all governments.[9] These interdependencies are further complicated because sharing takes different forms, i.e., sharing by program, such as grant-in-aid programs; sharing by politics, as in river and harbor improvement; and sharing by professionalization, through staff functions.[10] Obviously, there is no situation where one or others of those forms of sharing conditions excludes all others; more often they may be combined. Because in most cases the laws regarding a given governmental activity have not originated solely in one level of government, American law is not clear as to where responsibility lies and is thus a contributory factor in these interdependencies. Jeanne and David Walker consider the absence of guidelines as to which unit is best suited for which responsibility as a contributing factor for increased interdependency.[11]

Division of Activities

There is a continuing effort to determine which functions should be assigned to which level of government. At issue is the assignment of power and responsibility in accord with functions. Power over matters of policy, administration, and financing is distributed in an almost unlimited number of combinations among the levels of government and among functions. But decisions with regard to nearly all governmental functions are strongly influenced at the state level and meshed with related decisions made at the national and local levels. It is difficult to distinguish among the processes performed by the nation, state, or locality. One key lies in the fiscal process, where the unit at the higher level employs its greater access to financial resources but leaves actual utilization of the resources to the lower levels. Also, there are differences in constituencies between the various levels, and partial or functional constituencies such as the highway and education interests are frequently more powerful at the state than at other levels.[12]

Urbanization accentuates the questions concerning assignment and/or division of functions, for urbanization intensifies the kinds of tensions already present in federal systems. Urbanization places greater demands on government to provide services or undertake activities which previously could be left to private interests. People tend to blame state and local governments when they are dissatisfied with the services they receive, which in turn may lead to greater demands for national government intervention and a tendency to centralize power and weaken the role of state and local governments.[13]

THE STATE'S PIVOTAL ROLE IN FEDERALISM

We believe that the states are the pivotal level of government. They are constitutionally coequal with the national government and are, as Syed states, the "legal stewards" of local government. There is a noteworthy legal difference between the national and state governments: The national government's grant of powers is enormous, but it derives from the Constitution which came from a grant of powers by the original states. The states have plenary, or complete, powers as a result of their original sovereignty. We can readily observe that state powers are extremely wide in domestic affairs and are total with respect to local government, which has only such powers as are delegated by the state.

Theoretically, the states hold the means of reclaiming the powers of both the national and local governments because a two-thirds majority of the states can modify or even abolish the Constitution.[14] At this writing thirty states of the necessary thirty-four have passed resolutions calling for a constitutional convention to amend the United States Constitution. Although the convention is to consider an amendment requiring the federal government to maintain a balanced budget, many legal scholars believe that the entire Constitution might be rewritten at such a convention.

In that all local governments within the states are treated equally as "creatures of the states," the states can reorganize the structure of local government, limited only by their state constitutions. Although that may be neither practical nor likely, the doctrine that states are the source of authority from which all other governments are derived has influenced the evolution of the American system profoundly. Throughout our history the federal and local governments have had to go to court to justify expansion of activity and new undertakings not specifically sanctioned in their basic legal documents.

Nevertheless, even partisans of the states admit this power has been somewhat illusory.[15] States are constitutionally powerful, but generally they have been unwilling or unable to assume their "rightful role in the federal system."[16] The generally inactive way states have met with metropolitanization is often cited as an example of how states have neglected to use their powers. This "pivotal yet seemingly powerless" problem has received much attention in the past two decades. The states' capacity to function effectively as members of the federal partnership has been under assessment for many years. Both critics and supporters have developed arguments explaining why states have not reacted more vigorously to the challenges of metropolitanization. There are several arguments which give various perspectives on why states have not played a positive role in responding to the changing environment created by metropolitanization.

One argument posits that states have been unable to help their metropolitan areas because of self-imposed constitutional restrictions. State constitutions are unlike the U.S. Constitution in both scope and effect. The U.S. Constitution grants certain powers to the national government and reserves the rest of the powers to the states. State constitutions then cannot grant powers to the state since it already has them; rather, states can limit powers.[17] The state constitutions "limit powers even when they purport to grant them," because any definition of what powers an institution can use necessarily curbs that institution's power.[18] For example, when a state gives its governor powers, it is actually restricting a governor to using only the power it defines. Thus state constitutions are very complex instruments to deal with. At best they guard against infringement of basic values, and at worst they are impregnable, containing the fears and values of the past. Even though state constitutions frequently are difficult to amend, all laws must be consistent with them. This situation can be a major stumbling block if a state wants to aid its metropolitan areas because the constitution may contain limitations on the state's capacity to affect local government structures.

A second argument says states have not helped out metropolitan areas because they have had little desire to do so. Or, say critics of states, at the very least, the states have not kept pace with the attempts by the national and local governments to adjust to metropolitanization.[19] It is argued that states have not exercised their "rightful role in the federal system" because of gross deficiencies in their organization and procedures and that, because these problems are remediable by state action, states themselves are responsible for their failures to maintain coequal status. Although states command various resources including the wide reservoir of legal power, statewide jurisdiction, and access to diversified sources of money, their attention to the problems of the cities and the complexities of metropolitan areas has been limited. Only in the most recent years have any of the states made contributions to the programs designed to alleviate the problems of urban America. Again, the reason for lagging is seen as political, not constitutional. In support of this view it is argued that the reapportionment of states, which accorded urban areas more appropriate representation, occurred only under federal court order and even then many years too late to prevent the current problems. For by that time the balance of power had already shifted to the suburbs, leaving central cities in an ever-worsening position.

A third view holds that the states' past role in solving metropolitan problems has necessarily been a subtle one. Each of the fifty states has an identifiable consituency, but each individual state's visibility is submerged in the totality of the federal system.[20] Further, according to Willbern, state government has been generally less visible than the national or local governments because there are more nongovernmental constellations of power at this level.[21] He argues that interest groups exert more influence on the state capitol than is the case in Washington or at City Hall; therefore, individual states have little opportunity to assert broad initiatives to solve metropolitan problems whose solutions may have national implications. Even when an individual state does take important actions, they often go unrecognized because of the indistinctiveness of the state's urban policy. To the citizens and the media, states seem not to be as vital or closely attuned to the needs and values of the people as are other governments. Willbern goes so far as to say that they do not constitute economic and social entities to the degree that the national and local governments do.[22] The states have identities, but strong interdependence and lack of visibility seriously compromise whatever independent initiatives they may undertake to reverse or redirect the course of public policies.

A counterargument states that although accusations of inaction on metropolitan issues may be partially valid, states can point to some impressive recent accomplishments. As an example, it is pointed out that state aid to local government, and especially to large cities, has been increasing. The National Governors' Conference reports that states have moved to establish much closer and more viable working partnerships in the establishment of substate regional entities which stimulate citizen participation and assist local governments in combining resources for improving services.[23] Additionally, states are improving the quality of their performance by the use of sophisticated modern business methods and tools, including effective information management data systems.

In summary, it appears that states have, for a variety of reasons, not been aggressive in ameliorating the negative effects of metropolitanization. Instigated by various interests such as the poor, minorities, or developers and lending institutions, the federal government has taken the lead in assisting local governments. The federal government has established many programs of direct aid to localities which bypass the states themselves. If the states were not to take action on the problems of localities, then various groups looked to the federal government for action. The pendulum of intergovernmental relations began in the late 1970s to swing toward a position where the states have started to reenter the process of responding to urban areas.

Federal Impact on States and Localities

The great expansion of federal aid programs started during the Depression and accelerated again during the 1960s. There is little doubt that the national government went into the business of welfare on a wholesale scale because the states did not have the fiscal resources to do the job needed at that time. Their inability to relieve the human suffering caused by financial loss stemmed from the terrible force of the Depression on state finances, and not from legal, philosophical, or political questions. But the failure of state programs has not been the reason for the expansion of national programs, even though this is widely believed. The national government has at times entered a program arena because of the success of state programs. To see evidence of this, it is only necessary to go back and examine the origins of required health and safety standards in manufacturing and mining, the establishment of minimum wages, of unemployment compensation, of aid to the aged and blind, and the building of roads, to name but a few examples.

The fact that the national government has been playing a more visible role in metropolitan areas produces a changed political setting. Fears are often expressed that the states are being bypassed when large amounts of federal aid are passed directly to cities. It may be, however, that the growth of national aid programs has engendered a broader outlook and a greater professionalism among state administrators. By 1966, federal aid programs had a greater urban orientation than ever before; an increasing number of federal programs had enacted "we-will-act-if-you-don't" privisions; and the federal government had entered into new fields.[24] Cities and the national government both have exerted direct as well as indirect pressures on states to participate in federal programs, in which they are increasingly necessary and frequently willing partners.[25]

Future Revival of the States?

Strong state governments can strengthen the federal system by improving the balanced interactions of federalism. The increase in domestic spending by the states suggests an enlarged area of activity for them. When localities cease to deliver an adequate portion of the welfare and services that people want, the state may move to fill the vacuum.

Given the different ways states have been viewed in the past, it is important to ask what the states are doing now and what directions they might take. Metropolitan areas have problems that cannot be ignored indefinitely. Such problems can reach a crisis level before a state takes action. The major question to be addressed is whether states will be able to provide the necessary leadership. The way states handle the problems of metropolitan areas in the next decade will probably determine both the further development of metropolitan areas and the future of state government.

Several courses of action have been recommended for states. In an analysis of the 1967 New York constitutional convention, Donna Shalala suggests that as opposed to writing short permissive constitutions, the states should mandate directly the use of their resources by assuming functions, rewriting their aid formulas, and providing money and expertise.[26] She suggests that states become the metropolitan governments, an idea that is not new but which supports a conclusion of Meyerson and Banfield that the State of Massachusetts is becoming the equivalent of a metropolitan government for its eight metropolitan areas.[27]

The willingness of the state to assume additional fiscal responsibility, however, depends on the adequacy of its own finances as well as the distribution of political power between urban and rural legislators in the state legislature. A state may increase aid step by step, until the aid comes to represent a dominant proportion of the total funding of a service, and then the state may possibly assume full responsibility for that function. This course of action naturally means the state must be willing to assume heavier fiscal responsibilities. The process of transferring functions from local to state level is expected to be gradual, but this process is perceived as easier to accomplish than local government reorganization.[28]

The primary advantages of state assumption of a function are fiscal: resources can be equalized, money can be concentrated where it is needed most, and tax burdens can be better distributed.[29] The state has an additional advantage in possessing the authority to handle problems with a geographic scope exceeding that of local governments. On the other hand, disadvantages are evident in that state assumption can lead to overcentralization of decision-making power and may discourage local government from taking action on difficult problems. Thus state assumption of functional responsibilities could prove counterproductive. What may be more desirable is a jointly developed state-local policy that would systematically allocate authority over functions and their components among state, regional, and local governments.[30]

Although state assumption of services has potential risks of a political, economic, and administrative nature, some degree of increased state involvement in service delivery seems needed. At the same time, states need to allow local governments to experiment with their structures and their service delivery programs. The problems associated with metropolitanization not only vary among the fifty states, but also among urban areas within individual states. Increased state involvement does not necessarily mean decreased local involvement in responding to metropolitanization. The nature of the federal partnership is altered with states playing a more involved role along with the other levels of government.

Such an expanded role would allow states to use their greater access to financial resources to aid the cities, but should continue to leave the disposition of the money to the local governments. The idea here is akin to that underlying general revenue sharing or the current Community Block Grant program, where localities document their fiscal needs and then are able to use the resources they are given as they wish.

Another form of partnership would have the states allow and actively encourage local government to experiment with their governmental structures and service delivery systems. For example, the 1972 Montana Constitution contains a unique section that mandates a study of the existing form of government in every city, town, and county, even if there is no clear need for reform. The modernization mandate has so far resulted in two city-county consolidations, structural changes in four county governments, and two service consolidations. (See Chap. 4 for further discussion.)

Each of these alternative state initiatives has been utilized to some degree by some states. States have approved certain actions which would help solve the problems of local governments in metropolitan areas; but the number of these reforms has not been overwhelming, nor has the rate of reform increased appreciably in the last few years. One reason for this has been the depressed national economic condition of 1975-77, 1979-80, which led states to slowing expenditure increases and emphasizing "fiscal restraint" and "fiscal responsibility."

Although many states do not assume more service responsibilities because of the huge financial burdens involved, others have moved to reorganize the structure of local government or to enact innovative urban-related state programs. Massachusetts and Michigan traditionally have been the country's leaders in state urban policy. In 1978 California moved to join them with the initiation of an ambitious policy to revitalize inner cities and suburbs and to curb wasteful sprawl. Governor Jerry Brown endorsed an urban policy statement and forty-seven specific recommendations, with the goal of preserving agricultural land, increasing center-city employment, and enabling people to live closer to their jobs.

Looking back, we can see that the 1970s brought a reversal of the long period of state invisibility in the federal system as states reacted to the challenges of urban growth and technological advance. Many of the major industrial states became involved financially and administratively in the problems of local government, providing funds for such diverse functions as cleanup of polluted water, mass transit, and housing and urban development. Additionally, a start was made on structuring state government to meet the challenges of the times. As of 1980, thirty-nine states had established state departments of community or local affairs, and more than half had gone from biannual to annual sessions of their legislatures. Other changes have been in the form of legislative pay increases, provision of professional staffs, and the enlarged role of legislative leaders in implementing federal programs. These modernized legislatures are expected to be more responsive to the needs of metropolitan areas than past legislatures.

Components of the modernization agenda have also included authorizing one or more lengthened gubernatorial terms, reducing the number of independently elected officials in order to concentrate executive power in the governor, and granting permission for the governor to reorganize the executive branch, subject to veto of the legislature. With regard to the financial situation of the states, most now have a broad-based sales tax, and four-fifths have a personal income tax. The Walkers claim that "the political condition of the states in some respects has never been so salutary with more integrity, more openness, and greater two-party competition" than ever before, but the real test of a state's strength lies in its relationships with its localities.[31] If the states are to be "middlemen with muscle," not merely "middlemen with potential," their relationships with their localities will very likely have to change. They conclude that state-local relations today are better than they were in the past because of the "greater responsiveness, activism, assistance and assertiveness of the states."

If one examines the information on the growth of state governments during the past several decades it is difficult to give full credence to predictions of the states' demise. For example, the rate of growth for state governments since the end of World War II has been greater than that of the national government, and the number of state employees has doubled while national government employment of civilians has risen only slightly since 1950. Specifically, federal employment on a per capita basis has grown only 1.9% in the last twenty years; state employment meanwhile has grown 182%.[32] State governments spread more money, employ more people, deliver more services, and are more visible now than ever before. Nevertheless, there is a sense in which the states have declined in the balance of national and state leadership and in taking public policy initiatives. Whatever the growth potential is for the states, we do not fear for their disappearance. Among the comforting developments cited in the easing of intergovernmental tensions are the creation of the U.S. Advisory Commission on Intergovernmental Relations, the establishment of state departments of local affairs and offices for federal aid program coordination, increased authority of governors in budgeting, and the reapportionment of state legislatures.[33]

Thus far, reapportionment has chiefly benefitted suburban communities, though it may in the future aid metropolitan areas at large. If suburban interests continue to control powerful positions in state legislatures, we do not expect them to prod the state into structural change of metropolitan area governments. Rather, they will be more likely to oppose such suggestions. Only in southern and western areas have states used their authority to encourage and assist in the creation of new areawide units of government for metropolitan communities.

The metropolitan area is not yet a "creature of the state," but it could be a creature of the state, of the national government, of both, or of neither.[34]

STATE CONSTITUTIONS—LOCALITIES AS COMMUNITIES

States' Rights—"Whose Rights?"

A distinction between "states' rights" and "peoples' rights" exists in the Tenth Amendment: "The powers not delegated to the United States by the Constitution, nor prohibited by it to the States, are reserved to the States respectively, or to the people." Thus the Constitution that was developed gives rights to the people and power to the states; the central government was to have been restrained by the reservation of power for the states. The founding fathers wanted a limited government to allow maximum freedom for the people from that government. This "states' rights" doctrine is a reflection of the Jeffersonian theory about the sovereignty of the individual. According to Syed, Jeffersonians see government as evil because "it seeks to inhibit the individual who is sublime; in order that the individual may be free, the government must be shackled and paralyzed."[35]

Historically, most issues involving "states' rights" and the national government have been decided against the states. Such issues include state authority in interstate commerce, police power, voting rights, and, of course, the doctrines of nullification, secession, and interposition. On the other hand, the traditional theory of the states as unitary entities holds that the state governments can make decisions unilaterally within their boundaries regarding localities and the allocation of functions. Both state and federal courts as well as the Supreme Court have affirmed state power and authority on every occasion that the question has been adjudicated: based on Dillon's rule state powers are supreme and local governments are limited to those powers expressly delegated by state grant.

There is another doctrine which argues that states are quasi-federations of their localities and that the legal connections between states and localities parallel that of the national government and the states.[36] The origins of this theory lie in Anglo-Saxon tradition and in colonial times when the belief in the people's inherent right to local self-government was widespread. As Martin has pointed out, it was reinforced in the union of existing towns and was actually the origin for some of the states. Nevertheless, this theory has remained little more than a "legitimate constitutional heresy," a belief with some historical accuracy but without much force in law.

It is our view that neither of these theories fully embraces the relations between states and their localities. Problems associated with city and county home rule suggest that states are not federations of local governments, but the continual discussions over local powers suggest that the unitary concept also is incomplete. Elazar posits a third view--that the states should be considered unions of civil communities. A perspective of the states as a union of civil communities combines elements from several views. It differs from a unitary system in that its components do not simply exist at the discretion of the central polity; it differs from a federal system in that its components do not exist only as part of the larger whole with those powers as are authorized by the central polity.

Scholars traditionally have said that state constitutions have more often than not interfered with rather than advanced governmental functions and service delivery in urban areas.[37] One can point to specific constitutional provisions which acted against efficient and responsible government, such as restrictions on executive authority, restrictions on the state's ability to change local government structures, or boundaries, and limitations on state and local fiscal powers. Such restrictions on state governments hobble local governments as well, because the localities cannot look to the state for help in facing urban problems if the state has no capability to render it. But localities are most seriously restricted by the constitutional limitations on their own authority. Obviously, state constitutions and laws are the repository of the ground rules regarding urban and metropolitan affairs, and most of these are beyond the reach of national government to change. Nevertheless, local governments do provide the services residents desire in spite of state constitutional restrictions.

COMPETENCE OF GOVERNMENT: STATES

Theories of federalism which posit the rights and authorities of the various governments are just that: theories. Often the government that acts to resolve problems takes a large step toward creating its own authority. The right of government to exert its influence can be based upon whether it is effectively responding to a problem. This "competence of government" perspective argues that no governmental jurisdiction has a right to authority and power, that power has its own laws and that one of them is that it "abhors a vacuum."[38] The idea has been used as a way to explain to some degree the diminishing rights of the states. Today many officials agree that political inaction at the state level leads to takeovers by the national level, and that the competence theory applies to local government, too. Luther Gulick, one of the principal proponents of this theory, maintained that home rule municipalities have already lost, through incompetence, much of the content of their home rule to other governments.

The competence theory, as Syed suggests, may take the discussion of intergovernmental relations out of a more traditional framework of constitutional rights and into a framework of performance and accomplishment. If this theory is examined as part of the arena of power, success becomes the predominant criterion of judgment. Syed notes a tendency to accept the proposition that the ends justify the means. The argument does not reject outright the doctrine of local autonomy, because it is conceded that large competent municipalities may usefully exercise a measure of autonomy.

Local self-government is considered important because of its value as an obstacle to undue centralization, its usefulness as a means of political education, and the presumed superior ability of local citizens to understand their own needs and conduct their own business. Local self-government, however, requires not only sound intergovernmental collaboration and an involved body of citizens but also adequate governing powers, local jurisdictions of adequate size, and the availability of ways to change localities so as to meet new needs.

States are especially admonished for having failed to respond to the problems of urban America. But if states have responded poorly to urban problems, so have the national and local governments. Urban and metropolitan problems are so complex as to preclude easy assessments about the responsibilities of any government level. Before passing judgments, we need a more thorough understanding of what is involved in the metropolitan condition.

An attempt to define more precisely the metropolitan problems that need to be solved would be a natural starting place. Because demands in an urban area come from various groups, it matters who is doing the defining. Jobs and housing may be the problems to solve for the central-city poor, but the central-city middle class will see metropolitan tax inequities and crime as the major problems. Blacks who have gained some measure of local government power may see holding onto that power as the prime issue. The overriding issue for suburbanites may be the right to community self-determination. Pollution has become the cause for those who can afford the luxury of not having to be preoccupied with obtaining sufficient food, clothing, and shelter. J. Clarence Davies observes that concern for the problems of air and water pollution increases as one moves higher up the socioeconomic ladder.[39] Other groups may see transportation, health, or education as the most crucial problems in need of solution. The city is changing from a tight corporate community with specified services for its own citizens into a more ambiguous institution which supplies an indeterminate range of services to an amorphous constituency. This model of local government recognizes that most Americans are members of overlapping communities because it is difficult to attach their communal loyalties to one single unit of local government. If federalism has been advanced by forsaking concepts of strict division of power, then local government will be improved if there is less concern with jurisdictions and powers and more with cooperative arrangements and ad hoc shifts of responsibility.

And what of solutions? Reapportioned legislatures and the subsequent achievement of an equal voting power for residents of urban areas was hailed as a great victory for the cities. The prevailing opinion was that rural areas could no longer control legislatures and ignore urban problems. However, it is the opinion of many scholars that the decision to reapportion had been delayed too long; when it finally occurred, population growth in major central cities had passed its peak and the real beneficiaries of reapportionment became suburban areas. Additionally, recent decisions by the U.S. supreme Court regarding reapportionment as in Mahan v. Howell (1973) and Gaffney v. Cummings (1973) permit greater latitude in drawing reapportionment plans. Together with White v. Weiser (1973), they permit the states to enjoy a greater degree of autonomy in arriving at such distracting decisions.

Another solution called for is "metropolitanizing" the urban area. States are called on to require metropolitan areas to reform their fragmented systems of local government. But there are sharp disagreements among local people about what course of action should be followed, while many people do not want the state involved at all. A variation of this would have the states allow and actively encourage local government to experiment with their governmental structures and service delivery systems. As mentioned above, the 1972 Montana Constitution contains a unique government article that mandates a study periodically of the existing form of government in every city, town, and county, even if there were no clear need for reform.

Many courses of action are open to the states. One course would have the state use its resources to aid metropolitan areas directly by assuming local functions, a course of action that means the state must be willing to assume heavier fiscal responsibilities. The process of transferring functions from the local level to the state level would be gradual, but might be easier to accomplish than wholesale local government reorganization. Shifting functions would alleviate some of the problems of metropolitan areas because it would equalize resources, redistribute tax burdens, and provide more coordination of services.

As we have shown in this chapter, based upon their position in the federal relationship, the states have both the authority and resources to move in the direction of their own choosing in regard to metropolitan areas. That they may choose not to move at all, to continue with current patterns of relationships and nonrelationships, is also an obvious possibility. But it is impossible to deny the burgeoning presence and visibility of metropolitan areas within states all across the country and the capacity that the states have to deal with those areas.

NOTES

1. Daniel J. Elazar, "State-Local Relations: Reviving Old Theory on New Procedures," paper presented at the Fourth Annual Toward 1976 Conference, Chicago, October 1975, pp. 23-24.
2. Daniel J. Elazar, The American Partnership (Chicago: University of Chicago Press, 1967).
3. Morton Grodzins, The American System (Chicago: Rand McNally, 1966).
4. Daniel J. Elazar, "State-Local Relations," pp. 4-7.
5. Aaron Wildavsky and Jeffrey Pressman, Implementation (Berkeley: University of California Press, 1973).
6. Roscoe Martin, The Cities and the Federal System (New York: Atherton Press, 1965), p. 37.
7. Elazar, The American Partnership, p. 38.
8. Martin, The Cities and the Federal System, p. 38-39.
9. Grodzins, The American System, p. 11.
10. Ibid.
11. Jeanne Walker and David Walker, "Rationalizing Local Government Powers, Functions and Structures," States' Responsibility to Local Governments: An Action Agenda, National Governors' Conference, Washington, D.C., October 1975.
12. York Willbern, The Withering Away of the City (Bloomington: Indiana University Press, 1976), p. 74.
13. Daniel J. Elazar, "Urbanisms and Federalism," Publius 5, no. 2 (1975):37.
14. Herbert Kaufman, "Organization Theory and Political Theory," American Political Science Review, March 1974, p. 28.
15. Kaufman, "Organization Theory and Political Theory," p. 30.
16. Martin, The Cities and the Federal System, p. 46.
17. Frank P. Grad, "The States' Capacity to Respond to Urban Problems: The State Constitution," in The States and the Urban Crisis, ed. Alan K. Campbell (Englewood Cliffs, N.J.: Prentice-Hall, 1970), p. 29.

18. Ibid.
19. See Donna Shalala, The City and the Constitution (New York: National Municipal League, 1972); Willbern, The Withering Away of the City; Martin, The Cities and the Federal System; and Campbell, The States and the Urban Crisis.
20. Lee Green, Malcolm E. Jewell, and Daniel R. Grant, eds., The States and the Metropolis (University: University of Alabama Press, 1968), p. 22.
21. York Willbern, "The States as Governments in an Area Division of Powers," in Area and Power, ed. Arthur Maass (Glencoe, Ill.: Free Press, 1959), p. 74.
22. Willbern, "The States as Governments," p. 75.
23. National Governors' Conference, Innovations in State Government (Washington, D.C., June 1974), p. 4.
24. Daniel R. Grant, "The Decline of States' Reports and the Rise of State Administration," in Green, ed., The States and the Metropolis, pp. 104-8.
25. Martin, The Cities and the Federal System, p. 171-74.
26. Shalala, The City and the Constitution, p. 23.
27. See Meyerson and Banfield, Boston: The Job Ahead (Cambridge: Harvard University Press, 1966).
28. Alan Campbell and Roy W. Bahl, eds., State and Local Government: The Political Economy of Reform (New York: Free Press, 1976), p. 200.
29. John J. Callahan and Ruth M. Bosek, "State Assumption of Urban Responsibilities," in Campbell and Bahl, eds., State and Local Government.
30. Ibid.
31. Walker and Walker, "Rationalizing Local Government," pp. 113-15.
32. "The Real Big Government in the States," Washington Monthly, April 1978, p. 23.
33. Grant, "The Decline of States' Reports," pp. 113-15.
34. Ibid., p. 132.
35. Anwar Syed, The Political Theory of American Local Government (New York: Free Press, 1966), p. 50.
36. Elazar, "State-Local Relations," p. 14.
37. Grad, "The States' Capacity," p. 32.
38. Syed, The Political Theory of American Local Government, p. 138.
39. J. Clarence Davies, The Politics of Pollution (New York: Pegasus, 1970), p. 83.

Chapter 4

LOCAL GOVERNMENT FORMS AND FUNCTIONS

INTRODUCTION

There are approximately twenty-six thousand local governments in the nation's metropolitan areas. All twenty-six thousand were created by the states. Theoretically, the states can abolish or reorganize local governments as they choose. In practice, once local governments have been created, states do not act to abolish them. States have left the option of adopting governmental reorganization to the localities themselves. Rather, states expand or restrict the capacity of local government to act. State aid and technical assistance on the one hand, and state-imposed restrictions upon local government on the other, are commonplace.

    States do not usually impose major changes in local governmental structures upon localities. Rather, alteration in local governments, where it occurs, comes about through a joint state-local effort. Local governments may exert a great deal of political pressure upon states not to intervene too substantially. In part, state officials do not know any better than local officials what changes should be adopted.

    We would like to turn first to a brief discussion of the context of state-local government relationships. Then we will classify and describe the basic local governmental structures and examine some major attempts at altering governmental structures and boundaries. Finally, the major state-initiated procedural changes in local governmental operation will be discussed.

LOCAL GOVERNMENT IN A STATE CONTEXT

Most Americans do not reflect much on the differences in the local governments that surround them. If they live in the "corn belt," they notice that the county minds the roads; the township sees after the ballfields; the city provides hospitals; the special district takes charge of the water supply; and all of them, and states too, may supervise parks. These governments all provide increasing amounts of services. Since citizens do not often perceive the structural or procedural differences between city and county and special districts, and see only that the governments all function to deliver services, they remain largely unconscious of significant changes occurring in the role of local government.

Local governments have been and are created to deliver an increased number and level of services to specific geographical areas. Over the years, the way in which local governments have been created within metropolitan areas does not appear rational or logical. It can be and has been said that they are too many, too small, too big, too overlapping. Often they were created long before the impacts of urbanization were fully recognized. There has been a great deal of ongoing change--some would call it incremental change--in the adjustment of local governments to the needs of the urban population.

The states temper such changes either by satisfying the accelerating local demands for services by providing them, by authorizing the adaptation of local structures, or by providing guidance to localities adopting unfamiliar procedures. States have not, however, played a forceful initiating role in reorganizing local government to meet contemporary changes and challenges. Often there is disagreement on what functions should be performed by local governments or what problems are to be solved. States have been reluctant to alter local governmental structures. Thus established local governmental structures persist; they are difficult, often nearly impossible to abolish. The state rarely steps in to eliminate inadequately functioning local government, even though they are creatures of state authority. For one thing, the state does not often have standards to determine when a local government is inadequate; and for another, it only has the political power to force change upon such governments in crisis situations. Even villages which do not function and have no existing governmental activities are carried on the "books" as legal entities. Federal revenue sharing checks have on occasion been returned to the "sender" because of the difficulty of determining if a particular local government does, in fact, exist.

TYPES OF LOCAL GOVERNMENT

Local government, by definition, must (1) exist as an entity with organization and some corporate powers; (2) be governmental in character, meaning an agency of the public with elected or appointed officials; and (3) possess substantial autonomy, as exemplified by having a budget and access to revenue sources.[1] Despite their vast numbers and myriad forms, local governments can be classified into three categories--general-purpose corporate, general-purpose territorial, or special-purpose.

General-purpose Corporate Governments

Most corporate units are what we commonly think of as cities, e.g., central cities with large concentrations of population and economic diversity. Use of the term "city" is simply a nonlegal reference to a municipality, town, or village. Casual use of the term "suburb" implies an entity with limited economic functions and a large measure of homogeneity--a middle-class, white, residential suburb, for example. Municipalities are incorporated political subdivisions of the state which have been granted certain powers to provide urban service aspects of local government.

Legally subordinate to the state, municipalities are granted charters at the request of their inhabitants. When residents in a community find that they have certain interests that cannot be achieved individually or privately, they form a corporate community with legal rights and responsibilities to achieve those joint interests. The corporate community's rights transcend many individual rights such as unfettered use of one's land. An individual may wish to raise chickens in the backyard of a townhouse, but the corporate community will have enacted laws against that type of activity in order to protect the health of the community. Concern for the community's public health would override the individual's desire to build and maintain chicken coops.

Like any other corporation, public or private, the municipality can own property, make contracts, sue or be sued, and normally exists in perpetuity. Unlike a private corporation, however, the municipal corporation may exercise only such powers as are authorized under state law and can act only for public purposes. Towns, villages, and boroughs are types of municipalities that generally are less densely populated than cities. Boroughs are found in only four states: Connecticut, New Jersey, Pennsylvania, and Minnesota. The designation of "town" may or may not refer to a corporate entity, depending upon how the state defines "town." New York towns are corporate entities, whereas in midwestern states, township refers to a territorial subdivision of the county.

According to 1977 census data, as shown in Table 4.1, 18,862 of the 79,862 local governments in the nation are municipalities,

Table 4.1 Local Governments, by Type, 1942-1977

Type	1977	1972	1962	1952[a]	1942[a]	Percentage change, 1942-1977
Local governments	79,862	78,218	91,186	116,756	155,067	- 51.5
Counties	3,042	3,044	3,043	3,052	3,050	- 2
Municipalities	18,862	18,517	18,000	16,807	16,220	+ 16.3
Townships	16,822	16,991	17,142	17,202	18,919	- 11.1
Special districts	25,962	23,885	18,323	12,340	8,299	+313
School districts	15,174	15,781	34,678	67,355	108,579	- 86

[a] 1952 data adjusted to include units in Alaska and Hawaii: comparable data unavailable for 1942.

Source: Bureau of the Census, U.S. Department of Commerce, Governmental Organization, vol. 1., no. 1, Census of Governments (Washington, D.C.: U.S. Government Printing Office, 1978), pp. 12-14.

which is an increase of 16.3% over those existing in 1942. The creation of municipalities has thus been on the increase. Rather than eliminating cities, states have been creating them. Most of the cities created since 1967 have been in areas that have been undergoing metropolitanization.[2]

General-purpose Territorial Governments

Territorial local governments, on the other hand, are not chartered corporations. They are simply geographic units delineated by the state. All territory of the state is subdivided into subunits called counties. In effect, territorial local governments are subdivisions of the state created to deliver state services to the local level. The territorial boundaries thus cannot expand to meet the needs of local population growth. The boundaries of a county are always fixed unless a municipality diminishes the county land through annexation. Jefferson's plan for local self-government, followed in the Midwest, was to divide counties into 6-mile-square sections or "little republics" which would manage the roads, police, and welfare and also hold meetings on statewide concerns so as to provide guidance to the state.

Counties are an English governmental form adopted initially in the southern states. Existing in every state except Alaska, they are generally regarded as unimportant and perform few functions in the New England states. There is no typical county government, although many are still run by boards of commissioners which normally do not legislate. While counties were initially state administrative subunits, they are now taking on a dual role, especially in metropolitan areas, as their populations increasingly make service demands upon them. Often the county is the only existing local government for residents of unincorporated areas. Thus many counties in urban areas currently provide "city"-type services such as police protection, recreational facilities, planning, and libraries.[3] One indication that counties are more frequently becoming urban service providers is that seventy-six qualified for Community Development Block Grants from the federal government in the first year of the program. To become eligible, they had to be granted the power of eminent domain and to undertake urban renewal and publicly assisted housing programs. Thus counties, although territorial units, are coming to resemble cities in the services they provide, especially in metropolitan areas.

When urbanization patterns do not fit existing governmental structures, territorial units are forced to deliver more "corporate" city-type services. This leads to the hybrids, or the county-type area such as the city-counties, metropolitan governments, independent cities, or areas with county offices or governments organized on a regional basis. The Census Bureau has recently begun to use the designation of "urban county" for home-rule counties in which the jurisdiction has evolved from a rural, administrative arm of the state to a form resembling a municipality with legislative capacity and increased service delivery. The Census recorded 3044 counties in 1972, to which number the Advisory Commission on Intergovernmental Relations (ACIR) adds 101 county-type areas.[4]

In some states, particularly in the Midwest, the counties are further subdivided into townships. Townships are most evident in the north central states of the Midwest and the mid-Atlantic areas. As highly artificial government jurisdictions, they have boundaries that were originally marked out in a rectangular fashion by federal surveyors while the land was still part of the national domain. The functions of most have been restricted in number and are minor in nature. They are usually responsible for roads and one or two other functions. Some states have never established townships as a class of local governments. Rural townships have lost much of their vitality as their populations have declined. Yet urban townships have a somewhat brighter future as units of government, especially in certain suburban areas where metropolitan growth has occurred within townships.

Some states, such as Pennsylvania, have authorized urban townships to exercise many of the powers and provide many of the services normally reserved to municipalities; other strong townships states where such units have assumed major functional responsibilities are the six New England states and Michigan, New Jersey, New York, and Wisconsin. Townships have only minor responsibilities in ten states and do not exist in another twenty-nine. In 1977, the Census recorded 4031 townships in metropolitan areas. This represents a 16.4% increase from the 3462 in 1972.[5] In metropolitan areas the townships on the urban fringe, although territorial units, assume corporate characteristics and provide "city"-type services that their residents request.

The territorial form is not always sufficient to satisfy the residents' numerous interests. For example, traditional territorial counties, because they are not public corporations, cannot own property or incur debts. Thus if an urbanizing community in a territorial county wants water-sewer lines, its government cannot provide them because that would imply incurring a debt. The community has the choice of seeking to become a part of the city, which, as a corporation, can install and own water-sewer lines; it can attempt to incorporate itself; it can seek a change in its county's status; or it can establish a special district. Special districts are occasionally established precisely to circumvent such county fiscal constraints.

Special-purpose Governments

When general-purpose corporate or territorial units do not meet the needs of citizens, units of local governments known as special districts are created to satisfy one or a few specific such needs. They are a mix which is part territorial and part corporate. Generally, they are created by legislative authorization which may or may not be the result of citizen petition. Their functions range from the delivery of urban-type services such as parking, fire protection, water, or sewage to natural-resource-type activities such as soil conservation, flood control, or irrigation, and may also include providing miscellaneous services such as cemeteries and hospitals. While almost all types can impose some form of user charge, many are also authorized to levy taxes or special assessments against property. As Table 4.1 shows, the 1977 Census records 25,962 special districts, an increase of 300% from 1942, making this the fastest growing type of local government.

Part of the reason for the continued popularity of special districts is that they are being recognized as a partial solution to the problem of the regional delivery of more than one service. A new practice is to empower districts to perform a number of functions, making them multipurpose in character, in effect converting them into a form of general government. Consequently, areawide functions such as mass transportation, water and air pollution control, and port development have increasingly become the responsibilities of large regional special districts, as in the major urban areas of Atlanta, Boston, Chicago, New York, St. Louis, San Francisco, Seattle, and Washington, D.C. In some areas, multifunctional regional special districts have been established: Oregon legislation permits the establishment of multifunctional districts in metropolitan areas; Colorado legislation provides for the formation of service authorities that could provide more than one function on a regional or multicounty basis; and the Municipality of Seattle service district for sewerage has taken over the city and county bus system.

The school district is both the best known and most widespread form of special district. Fifteen thousand of the approximately 17,000 school systems, in the United States are independent school districts authorized to raise revenue and frame budgets within the conditions set by state law. Boundaries for many of the districts are the same as those of villages, towns, cities, or counties, while others have boundaries which extend into several of these jurisdictions. A dramatic decrease in the number of school districts has taken place over the last several decades. This was primarily due to consolidation of small school districts into larger districts which could offer a comprehensive program through high school. Educators who provided the impetus for the consolidation movement believed that college entrance required a comprehensive high school curriculum which only could be achieved in school districts that were large enough to offer specialized courses: science, mathematics, foreign language, etc. As Table 4.1 shows, the number of school districts decreased 54% between 1962 and 1972, and 86% between 1942 and 1972.

A form of local government closely akin to the special district is the so-called authority, as in the familiar New York Port Authority. It differs from a special district only in its fiscal base. Traditionally an authority has operated in a manner similar to a private corporation with a profit-making motive, authorized to issue revenue bonds but not to tax. This distinction between authorities and special districts is blurring as authorities are more frequently given public support and many special districts are authorized to issue revenue bonds. A major proportion of the authorities are established to serve regional and metropolitan transportation needs, as in airport, seaport, or highway development. The Washington, D.C. Metropolitan Area Transit Authority, for example, was created by state law and interstate compact to develop a metropolitan rapid-transit system for the Washington, D.C. area.

Overview of Local Government

Territorial, corporate, and special-district governments are all operating under increased pressure to deliver more services at an ever-increasing level of professionalization. Because of this pressure and for other reasons, corporate and hybrid governments have flourished to become what some call the "fragmented metropolitan governments" discussed in Chap. 2. Territorial governments, with their geographic basis, cover the nation. There will probably never be many more counties than there are now, save for the possibility of Alaskan boroughs subdividing or for an isolated successful effort at dividing a county in two.[6] Thus, since the number of territorial governments is not growing, the fragmentation of metropolitan areas clearly results from the proliferation of other forms, particularly special-purpose governments.

A brief review of Table 4.2 will illustrate the growth of local governments in metropolitan areas. The 264 officially designated Standard Metropolitan Statistical Areas (SMSAs) of 1972 contained 22,185 governmental units and 143,269,000 inhabitants. This means that there was one unit of government for every 6458 SMSA residents. By 1977 there were 272 SMSAs, with 25,869 governmental units for

Table 4.2 Number of Governmental Units in SMSAs, 1967 and 1977

	1977	1972[a]	1967[a]	Percentage change 1967-1977
SMSAs	272[b]	264	264	—
Counties	594	444	447	24.3
Municipalities	6,444	5,467	5,319	18.5
Townships	4,031	3,462	3,485	14.2
School districts	5,220	4,758	5,421	- 3.7
Other special districts	9,580	8,054	7,569	20.7
Total government units	25,869	22,185	22,241	14.2
Total population	154,655,000	143,269,000		

[a] Figures in this column are computed using the number of SMSAs which existed in 1972 in order to maintain consistency.
[b] The total number of SMSAs was increased to 272 in 1977. Thus, increases are in part due to additional units brought under the definition as well as the creation of new governments.
Source: Selected data from Advisory Commission on Intergovernmental Relations, Improving Urban America: A Challenge to Federalism (Washington, D.C.: U.S. Government Printing Office, September 1976), p. 11. That data came from Bureau of the Census, U.S. Department of Commerce, Census of Government, 1972, vol. 1, Governmental Organization (Washington, D.C.: U.S. Government Printing Office, 1973), and Bureau of the Census, U.S. Department of Commerce, Governmental Organization, vol. 1, no. 1, Census of Governments (Washington, D.C.: U.S. Government Printing Office, 1978), pp. 12-14.

154,655,000 people. As citizen demands in unincorporated areas increase, such areas create new local governments to meet service needs. As the figures in Table 4.1 show, the special district is the unit most relied upon to provide new services to urban residents in metropolitan areas.

As metropolitan areas expand, their existing governments and services do not expand to take in the new population and its needs, which would reduce the proportion of governments to people. Instead the governments existing in the newly metropolitanized areas persist, and, in fact, new ones, particularly special districts, are created to meet the growing demands of urbanization. The problem, in a nutshell, is that the scope of government does not keep up with the demographics of urbanization. Rather, the rate of increase in the number of governmental units outruns the rate of population increase, as indicated in Table 4.2. As the 264 SMSAs of 1972 grew to 272 in 1977, the population covered by them increased by 7.9% while the number of governmental units within them increased by 16.6%, with special districts leading at 18.9%. (Adjusting these figures by the 3% increase in number of SMSAs does not substantially alter the argument.)

STRUCTURAL AND BOUNDARY CHANGES IN LOCAL GOVERNMENT

Reform studies of metropolitan areas have given vogue to the concept of "rational" reassignment of the dozens of governmental functions and services to the "best" level of each activity. Reform may then be pursued by realigning the governmental institutions in metropolitan areas to fit the reassigned activities. There are at least two aspects of reform which must be kept in mind before calling for a complete reorganization of government in metropolitan areas. First, focusing only upon a rational reorganization of metropolitan government is restrictive. This leaves out a whole realm of alternatives, including public policy which is actually made within existing government structures and functions.[7] Second, the metropolitan reform approach ignores the fact that decentralized local structures are valuable objects of study by themselves apart from the services they deliver. Local governments may, after all, actually be responsible and give representation to the preferences of their residents as they are currently constituted.

Whether consolidated urban governments can, in fact, adequately meet the needs of diverse metropolitan populations is a very real question. Some observers maintain that decentralized government, with its greater emphasis upon local control, may be beneficial in the decision-making, administrative, legislative, and judicial concerns of metropolitan populations. Interest in maintaining decentralized government involves more than the facile conclusion that people desire a market basket of services to be provided at the metropolitan level. Many residents prefer smaller, more personalized governments even if services could be provided more efficiently by larger governments.

At a fundamental level, governmental centralization and decentralization reflect the basic question of how close government should be to its citizens and who should have control over local government. Metropolitan populations are diverse. There are both metropolitanwide concerns that affect all residents of the area and more localized concerns where subgroups vary widely on what they want local government to provide. State actions have begun to mirror this greater awareness of the attributes of decentralization through the establishment of substate districts. Whatever the direction, whether centralization or decentralization, the states are in a position to enact far-reaching changes.

Centralization

The pattern of government in metropolitan areas has generally been one of a mixture of a large central city and numerous other cities, counties, townships, special districts, and so forth. Since the 1920 Census first documented the growth of metropolitan areas, suburbs have grown faster than the central cities, and this trend has steadily continued with ever more people living in suburbs than in central cities. The population trends are reinforced by the number and density of governmental units in metropolitan areas which suggests to reformers the need for coordination because urban problems do not coincide with governmental boundary lines. Reformers have combatted local governmental crises and problems since the 1870s. First they campaigned for internal local governmental reforms which led to city-manager governments, nonpartisan elections, and merit personnel systems. Then reformers turned their attention to external structural change. Maxey wrote in 1922: "The great problems which demand governmental action in metropolitan communities--public health, recreation, public utilities, crime, and the like, hold political boundaries in contempt."[8]

This argues for reform via centralization of government, which necessitates a rearrangement of political units in an area. Unlike the relatively simple reassignment of services, reassignment of basic authorities amounts to altering the powers of government. When powers are shifted upward to metropolitanwide governments through centralization, the powers of all local governments are affected.[9] Understandably, centralization is a sensitive subject that states have preferred to leave in the hands of their localities. We would like to discuss three of the most widely attempted approaches to centralization in metropolitan areas: annexation of unincorporated areas; consolidation of cities and counties; and federation of existing incorporated areas, often referred to as two-tiered government.

Annexation Annexation of unincorporated territory has been, by far, the most utilized mechanism for centralizing government in metropolitan areas. It is a legal procedure whereby municipal boundaries are expanded to incorporate additional unincorporated territory. Most of the country's cities achieved their current size through annexation. Table 4.3 shows that the largest cities have grown through municipal annexation. Between 1960 and 1970, two-thirds of all municipalities over 1,500 population annexed land. During that period of time, the areas annexed contained 6.6 million people. This figure represents more growth in population than occurred through the national increases of population in cities. Prior to the mid-nineteenth century, none of the American cities had a large population, but after the Civil War, immigration coupled with industrialization caused stunning growth in cities in the East and in the Midwest. The practice of acquiring large areas of nonurbanized land through annexation became very common. In the East and Midwest before 1900, annexation was usually achieved by state legislation or city council action, or by approval of a majority of the combined vote of the city and of the territory to be annexed.[10]

From the turn of the century until the end of World War II, an alliance of suburban and rural interests in legislatures generally made it harder for existing cities to annex than for new ones to incorporate independently, and the popularity of the former practice declined. In various states, legislatures passed more restrictive annexation laws, gave up their prerogatives to pass such special legislation, and allowed fringe area residents a voice in the process, which usually meant resistance to annexation. The resurgence in the popularity of the procedure after 1945 can be attributed to continued population growth in metropolitan areas and continued public resistance to governmental reorganization along more centralized lines.

Annexation helps cities prevent decreasing tax bases, further governmental fragmentation, and growing disparities among communities; it helps suburban fringe residents by providing the "city" services they increasingly need. By adding only such fringe areas, annexation thus does not really amount to wholesale governmental centralization of the entire metropolitan area. But because it seems to threaten something akin to centralization, annexation has declined in popularity more recently. Thus central cities are hemmed in. Central cities are hemmed in by incorporated communities whose residents, when the state allows them a voice in the matter, do not want to join the central city because they fear higher taxes, loss of identity, or political domination. On the other hand, blacks, gaining a political hold in many central cities, do not wish to dilute that power by annexation of white suburban voters. Some cities are reluctant to assume the expense of expanded services, while in some suburban areas service delivery is perceived as already adequate.

Table 4.3 Land Area, Population, and Density of Territory Annexed to Central Cities of 50,000 or More by Region and Size Group, 1950-1960 and 1960-1970

Classification	Total number of cities	Land area, 1970 (sq mi)	Population, 1970 (000)	Territory annexed, 1950-1960				Territory annexed, 1960-1970				Population when annexed	
				Land area, 1960 (sq mi)	Population, 1960 (000)	Population per sq mi, 1960	Land area, 1970 (sq mi)	Population, 1970 (000)	Population per sq mi, 1970	Total (000)	Population per sq mi	Percentage 1970 population
Total, central cities	260	15,028	61,956	3,119	5,092	1,633	4,599	3,746	815	2,454	534	65
Geographic region												
Northeast (including Del., Md., D.C., W. Va.)	64	1,873	18,833	29	25	849	46	32	688	23	500	73
North central	70	3,530	16,664	525	943	1,796	1,068	1,013	948	711	666	70
South (excluding Del., Md., D.C., W. Va.)	83	6,949	15,435	1,949	2,719	1,395	2,833	1,922	678	1,353	478	70
West	43	2,676	11,024	616	1,405	2,281	652	780	1,196	367	563	47
Population group												
Over 50,000	29	5,489	33,109	866	1,484	1,714	1,660	1,120	675	867	522	77
250,000-500,000	26	3,029	8,773	739	1,271	1,719	1,329	868	653	582	438	67
100,000-249,999	71	3,075	10,205	660	963	1,460	741	795	1,073	531	717	67
50,000-99,999 by 1950	62	1,333	4,404	249	283	1,137	198	158	798	80	404	51
50,000-99,999 by 1960	41	1,445	3,602	511	886	1,735	378	370	980	149	394	40
50,000-99,999 by 1970	31	657	1,863	94	205	2,176	293	435	1,485	245	836	56

Source: Advisory Commission on Intergovernmental Relations, Improving Urban America: A Challenge to Federalism (Washington, D.C.: U.S. Government Printing Office, 1976), p. 152. Reproduced from Municipal Year Book 1975, pp. 23, 24, and based on a compilation of city land areas for 1950, 1960, and 1970, drawn mainly from published Census data but rounded to the nearest whole square mile with some corrections to increase intercensal comparability. City population data are taken from the decennial Census volumes, and the densities have been computed from the compiled area and population data.

Nevertheless, southern and western cities have continued to grow by the process of annexation. Between 1960 and 1970, major southern cities almost doubled their average land areas by annexation while municipal boundaries in major northern areas remained virtually unchanged.[11] Nearly every southern central city which experienced population growth during the 1960s did so as a result of annexation. Significant growth through annexation in the last two decades was found in Oklahoma City, which went from 51 square miles to 648 square miles; Phoenix, from 17 to 248 square miles; Memphis, from 104 to 204 square miles; and Houston, from 160 to 426 square miles.[12]

Annexation thus affects more territory and population than any other reorganization approach. Yet annexation is a continuous and piecemeal approach to centralizing government in metropolitan areas. It is virtually unused as a centralizing method in the East and Midwest, while in the South and West cities annex rural areas as well as suburbs.

Consolidation Consolidation of government units occurs as mergers between counties, or between cities, or between cities and counties. In consolidation, one government is created to exercise all or most governmental powers for the area and thereby replace one or several of the existing governments. There is a continuing interest in city-county consolidation as a means for providing urban services and resolving metropolitan problems. But the idea is not a new one. A number of city-county consolidations took place during the nineteenth century. These included the merger of the City of New Orleans and the County of Orleans in 1805; the merger of the City of Boston with Suffolk County in 1882; the merger of the City and County of Philadelphia in 1854; and the merger of New York and Brooklyn and the counties of Queens and Richmond in 1898. The merger of the City and County in Honolulu was effected by the territorial legislature in 1907. All of these consolidations were the result of legislative enactment, and none required local citizen referenda.

No new city-county consolidations took place in the twentieth century until 1947. During the early years of the twentieth century, municipal reformers wrested from the state legislatures the power to make decisions about the structure of local government. An unforeseen side effect of such reform was the establishment of requirements for constitutional amendments and/or referendum elections as a basis for restructuring local government. These requirements make the achievement of city-county consolidations very difficult in that subpopulations have "veto" rights over the outcome via referenda.

City-county referenda: the record to date—In the last three decades there have been sixty-eight city-county consolidation referenda. Table 4.4 lists the referenda and the level of electoral support.

70 / Local Government Forms and Functions

Table 4.4 Voter Support for City-County Consolidation Referenda by Region, 1945-1976

Region	Year	Reorganization Referendum	Reorganization support (%) Adopted	Reorganization support (%) Rejected
Northeast	—	—	Subtotal —	Subtotal 0
North central	1959	Cleveland-Cuyahoga County, Ohio	0	44.8
	1962	St. Louis-St. Louis County, Mo.		27.5
		St. Louis-St. Louis County, Mo.		40.1[a]
	1974	Evansville-Vanderburgh County, Ind.		26.1
			Subtotal 0	Subtotal 4
South	1947	Baton Rouge-East Baton Rouge Parish, La.	51.1	
	1948	Miami-Dade County, Fla.		45.4
	1952	Hampton-Elizabeth County, Va.	88.7	
	1953	Miami-Dade County, Fla.		49.2
	1954	Albany-Dougherty County, Ga.		33.0
	1957	Miami-Dade County, Fla.	51.0	
		Newport News-Warwick, Va.[b]	66.9	
	1958	Nashville-Davidson County, Tenn.		47.3
	1959	Knoxville-Knox County, Tenn.		16.7
	1960	Macon-Bibb County, Ga.		35.8
	1961	Durham-Durham County, N. Car.		22.3
		Richmond-Henrico County, Va.		54.0[c]
	1962	Columbus-Muscogee County, Ga.		42.1

Structural and Boundary Changes / 71

	Memphis-Shelby County, Tenn.		36.8
	Nashville-Davidson County, Tenn.	56.8	
	South Norfolk-Norfolk County, Va.	66.0	
	Virginia Beach-Princess Anne County, Va.	81.9	
1964	Chattanooga-Hamilton County, Tenn.		19.2
1967	Jacksonville-Duval County, Fla.	64.7	
	Tampa-Hillsborough County, Fla.		28.4
1969	Athens-Clarke County, Ga.		48.0
	Brunswick-Glynn County, Ga.		29.6
	Roanoke-Roanoke County, Va.		66.4[c]
	Winchester-Frederick County, Va.		31.9
1970	Charlottesville-Albermarle County, Va.		28.1
	Columbus-Muscogee County, Va.	80.7	
	Chattanooga-Hamilton County, Tenn.		48.0
	Tampa-Hillsborough County, Fla.		42.0
	Pensacola-Escambra County, Fla.		42.0
1971	Augusta-Richmond County, Ga.		41.5
	Charlotte-Mecklenburg County, N. Car.		30.5
	Tallahassee-Leon County, Fla.		41.0
	Bristol-Washington County, Va.		17.5
	Memphis-Shelby County, Tenn.		47.6

[a]St. Louis-St. Louis County portions of the 1962 statewide referendum.
[b]Warwick, Va. was a city at the time of the referendum. It had incorporated in 1952; it was Warwick County just six years prior to the referendum. A similar situation preceded the consolidation of Suffolk and Nansemond cities.
[c]The type of majority requirement is vital in consolidation referenda. In these instances city-county consolidation was not possible despite majority voting percentage in its support.

Table 4.4 (Continued)

Region	Year	Reorganization Referendum	Adopted	Rejected
South (Cont.)	1972	Fort Pierce–St. Lucie County, Fla.		36.5
		Athens–Clarke County, Ga.		48.3
		Macon–Bibb County, Ga.		39.6
		Suffolk–Nansemond County, Va.b	75.7	
		Lexington–Fayette County, Ky.	69.4	
	1973	Tampa–Hillsborough County, Fla.		42.0
		Columbia–Richland County, S.Car.		45.9
		Savannah–Chatham County, Ga.		58.3c
		Tallahassee–Leon County, Fla.		45.9
		Wilmington–New Hanover County, N.Car.		25.6
	1974	Augusta–Richmond County, Ga.		51.5c
		Durham–Durham County, N.Car.		32.1
		Charleston–Charleston County, S.Car.		40.4
	1975	Ashland–Catlesttsburg–Boyd County, Ky.		16.7
	1976	Tallahassee–Leon County, Fla.		45.1
		Macon–Bibb County, Ga.		38.0
		Augusta–Richmond County, Ga.		45.5
	1978	Subtotal	11	Subtotal 40
West	1959	Albuquerque–Bernalillo County, N.Mex.		30.0
	1969	Carson City–Ormsby County, Nev.	65.1	
		Juneau–Greater Juneau Borough, Alaska	54.1	

Structural and Boundary Changes / 73

1971	Sitka–Greater Sitka Borough, Alaska	77.2	
1973	Albuquerque–Bernalillo County, N. Mex.		44.1
1974	Portland–Multnomah County, Ore.		27.5
	Sacramento–Sacramento County, Calif.		24.9
1975	Salt Lake City–Salt Lake County, Utah		39.0
	Anchorage, Glen Alps, Gerdwood–Greater Anchorage Borough, Alaska	60.2	
1976	Anaconda–Deer Lodge County, Mont.	56.2	
	Butte–Silver Bow County, Mont.	62.0	
	Missoula–Missoula County, Mont.		46.0
	Moab–Grand County, Utah		21.0
	Subtotal	6	7
		17	51

Total outcome

Total local reorganizations attempted = 68

[b]Warwick, Va. was a city at the time of the referendum. It had incorporated in 1952; it was Warwick County just six years prior to the referendum. A similar situation preceded the consolidation of Suffolk and Nansemond cities.

[c]The type of majority requirement is vital in consolidation referenda. In these instances city-county consolidation was not possible despite majority voting percentage in its support.

Note: There is currently no centralized recordkeeping for consolidation activity. This table was compiled from local reports on consolidation and consolidations reported in national journals such as the National Civic Review (New York: National Municipal League) and the National Association of Counties, County News (Washington, D.C.: National Association of Counties).

74 / Local Government Forms and Functions

The table illustrates the following generally held notions concerning reorganization efforts:

1. The large majority of reorganization attempts are rejected. Out of the sixty-eight attempts, seventeen have been ratified, giving an adoption rate of 25%.
2. Consolidation continues to be a single-county phenomenon.
3. The majority of attempts are made by medium-sized and small urban areas. Fifty-four of the sixty-eight attempts since 1947 (79%) have occurred in areas with central cities of 250,000 or less at the time of the referendum. In fact, eight attempts have taken place in areas with a central city of less than 10,000.
4. City-county consolidation is a regional phenomenon. There have been no adoptions in the Northeast or the north central states. Consolidations have centered in the South and more recently in the West.
5. Most adoptions are influenced by special indigenous factors that are not applicable elsewhere. Thus, for example, the Jacksonville-Duval consolidation was spurred on by criminal indictments of government officials.
6. Even though three-fourths of the proposals fail, a relatively stable number of them continue to be brought before the voters. The fact that many other areas consider consolidation without ever reaching the voting stage illustrates its continuing attraction.

The few adoptions that have occurred took place mainly in small urban environments, stimulated for the most part by unique circumstances. Consolidations, in sum, affect a very small proportion of the nation's urban population.

Consolidation: what's in a name?—The name implies complete consolidation of city and county, but actually, city-county consolidation charters voted upon are only partial reorganizations. Usually, existing municipalities, school districts, and special districts are excluded, and new special services and taxing districts are created as part of the consolidation charter. What appears to the casual observer to be complete consolidation more often resembles a multitiered structure for delivering services, with the county as an upper tier and municipalities or special service districts as lower tiers. Also, there remains a multiplicity of overlapping jurisdictions in addition to the county and small cities, including school districts and other special districts. Several examples illustrate the decentralization that still exists after consolidation.

The Nashville-Davidson, Tennessee case represents a classic example of consolidation often emulated by areas considering reorganization. The governments of the City of Nashville and Davidson County merged, thereby reducing fragmentation both vertically (by putting a "metropolitan" mayor at the head of the consolidated government) and horizontally (by making control over schools a metropolitanwide affair). Like most efforts at city-county consolidation, the Nashville metropolitan government contains local structures. For example, there exist two service areas, a generalized service district for the entire metropolitan district and an urban service district covering the old city of Nashville. Also, all the pre-1962 suburban municipalities resisted consolidation and have remained as functioning local governments.

Unigov, as the Indianapolis-Marion County consolidation is called, is also a very partial reorganization; it changed the complexities of government in the metropolitan area very little. The police and sheriff department remained separate, the schools remained locally controlled, several suburban municipalities resisted consolidation, and several important administrative organizations continued unaffected by consolidation. There still remain over two hundred local governments in the Indianapolis metropolitan area.

The term "city-county consolidation" has stuck. The literature makes reference to consolidation attempts since before the turn of the century. Yet many recent consolidations more closely resemble multitiered models, such as Miami-Dade County, than they do the more complete 1854 consolidation of Philadelphia. Multitiered models have been utilized because they are more politically palatable. Many of the consolidations subsequent to 1970 seem to avoid using the term "consolidation." "Consolidation" is not only an emotion-laden term which generates opposition to any major reorganization, but in most cases it is also an inaccurate description.

State-directed consolidation—Reversing the twentieth-century pattern of voter-approved mergers, the Indiana General Assembly created a consolidated government out of the merger of the City of Indianapolis and Marion County in 1969, returning in effect to the nineteenth-century pattern of legislative action. This change was made without any provision for a local referendum. In only the second consolidation since World War II to be accomplished by a legislature without the vote of the people, the Nevada Legislature in 1975 passed a Metropolitan Cities Incorporation Law and an Urban County Law providing for the consolidation of Las Vegas and Clark County, effective January 1977. However, the law was challenged and the consolidation overturned by the Nevada Supreme Court, which found that in mandating the consolidation, the Legislature had violated the state constitutional prohibition of special legislation.

The examples of Indiana and Nevada do not necessarily signify a trend to greater state leadership in consolidation efforts. They do, however, illustrate that consolidation is an issue which is being reconsidered as an organizational alternative by some states. We suspect states will give greater attention to consolidation, as well as other approaches to reorganization, as progress reaches a stalemate at the metropolitan level. The requirement of local referenda has made major structural change at the metropolitan level difficult if not impossible to achieve. Several states have exhibited awareness of this and have moved to facilitate structural change at the metropolitan level.

Federation Because proposals for consolidated government met with defeat so often and on so widespread a basis, scholars and practitioners have looked to additional alternatives that might still accomplish the centralization goals. Two-tiered federated government has been espoused by many as the most desirable approach to metropolitan reorganization.[13] Theoretically, in such a system, the central government would provide economies of scale and coordination, and the second tier of local governments would allow for citizen access and responsiveness to citizen needs. The basic concept of multitiered metropolitan government is the decentralization of some functions, the centralization of others, and the sharing of responsibilities.

At the metropolitan level, the federation can take three possible forms.[14] The first is a structure which is centered in the county, either through evolution or statutory enactment. Here a federated entity evolves by default, as the county government assumes growing powers or is increasingly given authority to deliver urban-type services. Approximately 170 SMSAs are made up either wholly or predominantly of one county, and in 100 of those county boundaries are coterminous with those of the SMSA.

Although there have been several attempts to create, through a single decision, a federation with the county at its heart, only one of these has been successful--the Miami-Dade County federation. The 1957 Dade County Charter referendum created the atypical Metropolitan Dade County Government.[15] It is a federated areawide government encompassing twenty-six municipalities in the county. Although the new county appropriated responsibility for a substantial number of services, the cities--called the "lower tier" of government--do continue to exist and to provide some services.

The second type of structural arrangement based on the federation principle is the Toronto-type metropolitan federation. In this case, unilateral action of the provincial legislature created a federated metropolitan government with two tiers. The new or areawide level was created, where none existed before, to encompass the municipality of Toronto and twelve immediately surrounding municipalities, the first-tier jurisdiction. Thus, in January 1954, an urban federated municipality unlike any in the United States came into existence. The Municipality of Metropolitan Toronto exercises areawide powers over metropolitan-scale functions while allowing the local jurisdictions to continue control over local functions and subfunctions. The thirteen constituent jurisdictions of Toronto were converted to six in 1967.

The third type of structural arrangement based on the federation principle is the state-supported areawide regional council. Examples of this approach are the Twin Cities Metropolitan Council and the Atlanta Regional Commission. In the Minneapolis-St. Paul, Minnesota area, the Twin Cities Metropolitan Council is a seven-county area planning agency established in 1967 by the state legislature, with its members appointed by the governor from fifteen districts. Possessing legislative drafting authority, the council guided the establishment of one of the few areawide taxes in the country. Although the council was given extensive administrative and decision-making responsibilities, it operates no services directly. The Atlanta Regional Commission, established in 1971, also incorporates the power to prepare comprehensive guides for planning and to review all area plans of constituents for conformity to guidelines. The primary characteristics of this type of federation is that the newly created second tier is predominantly a policymaking level while service delivery functions remain at the level of local governments in the region. The council influences service delivery through its authority to review all local government plans and veto powers.[16] Neither of these systems is in fact a general-purpose government, yet they are entities established on the federation principle that have great potential in metropolitan areas. They further illustrate state involvement in reorganizing metropolitan government.

Decentralization

At general election time, the efforts directed at centralizing government make the headlines as voters decide the issues of annexation, consolidation, and federation. Such efforts make the newspapers because they are unusual actions, while decentralization in government is the norm and a fact of life in metropolitan America. Decentralized local self-government is a foundation of American history, often called "grass roots government," and represents a tradition to which the citizenry feels strong attachment.

In light of the numerous unsuccessful attempts at centralization, it is clear that many Americans concur in one or more of the arguments

78 / Local Government Forms and Functions

for maintaining multiple units of local government. Among these are the ideas that (1) other values override concerns for economy and efficiency; (2) there is no single metropolitan community with which citizens feel an identity or sense of community; (3) it has not been proven that the core city subsidizes the suburbs; and (4) citizens today feel very strongly about the desirability of community and minority control. This attitude exists despite the numerous problems of noncentralization cited since the 1930s which have not diminished in the meantime, including inequitable tax burdens, fiscal chaos, frustration of popular control, and general difficulties in metropolitan areas.

Numerous observers of decentralization have examined the concept as a theoretical idea as well as a workable device for governance and administration.[17] According to Fesler, decentralization is a generic term for all types of power distribution.[18] Proponents of decentralization focus their efforts on decentralizing the central city of the metropolitan area discussed in the centralization section. A few large and powerful suburban counties could also qualify as targets. Whenever local government has gotten too removed from its citizens, either by choice or state fiat, the decentralists rally, seeking varying degrees of citizen participation in order to achieve neighborhood controls. As Hallman notes, "one of the most significant events bearing on public administration in recent years has been the demand by residents of urban neighborhoods for a greater voice in the programs which affect their lives."[19]

Triggered by the civil rights movement of the 1960s, the issue of governmental and bureaucratic responsiveness to citizen demands has been foremost and continuing. The 1968 reports of the National Advisory Commission on Civil Disorders (Kerner Commission) and the National Commission on Urban Problems (Douglas Commission) recommend establishing neighborhood outlets, decentralizing municipal services, and improving the delivery of services. According to Victor Jones, the challenges to the 1970s was still, exactly as in the 1960s, "to develop a system of government and politics which will deliver goods and services and administer regulations efficiently, effectively and justly, and at the same time provide, through representation and citizen participation, genuine popular control of the direction of governmental activity and a sense of communal membership.[20]

In recent years, as many scholars and practitioners alike have had "second thoughts" about the value of centralizing local governments, they have accepted the striking truth that there are maximum sizes for every organization, beyond which growth can only produce a reduction in efficiency. The political economy or public choice approach, while opposing consolidation, does not necessarily recommend decentralization, which might quite logically be considered the reverse side of the coin. Although not "decentralism" per se, the political economy approach has some affinity with the move toward metropolitan decentralization. As articulated by Bish, Ostrom, Warren, and others, the argument is that there is no one best size nor one best way to deliver public goods and services, but that a governmental system of multiple, overlapping jurisdictions can take advantage of diverse economies of scale for different public services. A public economy composed of multiple jurisdictions is likely to be more efficient and responsive than a public economy organized into a single areawide monopoly.[21]

In sum, there is a strong commitment on the part of citizens and some scholars to decentralize local governments in metropolitan areas. This has not manifested itself in a major movement to decentralize existing local governments. Rather it has reinforced the attachment of citizens to existing noncentralized governmental patterns of local government in metropolitan areas. The local government centralists and decentralists each have exerted sufficient pressure that major changes in governmental structure do not appear likely in either direction. States have received no clear mandate to centralize or decentralize local governments in metropolitan areas. States have concentrated most of their efforts on procedural and fiscal assistance to aid existing local structures.

PROCEDURAL CHANGES: STATE-INITIATED

In many states, officials have either reluctantly or willingly accepted the structure and arrangements of local governments in metropolitan areas as a given. Because of constitutional limitations or the difficulty of enacting massive legislative change, state officials, both administrators and legislators, have devised various methods to assist in the coordination of service delivery and other activities of local governments, especially in metropolitan areas. These devices include the creation of state departments or urban affairs; the encouragement of interlocal cooperation through regional councils; the fostering of contracts, compacts, or joint service agreements; functional transfers between localities, special districts, or subordinate service authorities; extending extraterritorial jurisdiction for cities; increasing home rule for counties and other county modernizations; and state aid increases. In this section we will look at examples of this trend in the form of state-mandated local boundary commissions and state-authorized cooperative agreements, contracts, and regional arrangements.

Local Boundary Adjustment Boards

In seven states, legislatures have established permanent bodies to exercise discretionary authority in such matters as reviewing petitions, initiating proposals, offering advice, and making determinations relating to boundary adjustments.[22] Discretionary boundary adjustment boards are either state boards or county or regional commissions in Michigan, Minnesota, Iowa, and Alaska. In the West Coast states of Washington, Oregon, and California, legislation in the 1960s authorized continuing boundary adjustment boards at the county or metropolitan levels.

The boards in each of the seven states are authorized to approve or disapprove proposals for annexation or incorporation, or alter the proposals before them. Except in California, the states also play roles in municipal consolidations and mergers. In a study of such agencies, Swanson found that their activities vary greatly in quantity and kind. Iowa's statewide commission has had little effect on boundary change. In Alaska, the boundary commission received generous constitutional authority but lacked strong backing from the legislature or the public.

Although the role of boundary commissions has been viewed, on the basis of their authority to review proposals, as a negative one, a more positive role in guiding local government growth is now emerging among them.[23] They are encouraging or requiring cities to develop sphere-of-influence plans for the areas which the city may expect eventually to annex. In California, Oregon, and Minnesota, the commissions are encouraging such a procedure so that cities and fringe areas can better plan for program activity and service delivery.

It appears likely that this form of state-local interaction is here to stay. None of the commissions that have been started has been disbanded. In a 1973 package of reform proposals relating to state and local relations, the ACIR recommended that states establish "broadly representative local government boundary commissions at the state and/or local levels" with a range of responsibilities, including that of providing leadership in boundary planning.[24]

Cooperative Service Agreements

The intergovernmental agreement is perhaps the oldest and the most popular type of procedure used for meeting metropolitan area and local government needs. In form, such an agreement may involve the decision between two or more governments to pursue a parallel or common course of action. It may take the form also of an informal agreement to improve services. More commonly, intergovernmental agreements are legal authorizations used to provide for the cooperative performance of a service by two or more local government units, or to provide by contract for the performance of a service by one government unit for one or more other such units. Such agreements, not necessarily permanent, more often pertain to services than to facilities. They may be established with or without voter approval, and they may provide for services either to the citizen or the government unit.

This type of cooperative approach has received support from local organizations, states, and the national government. States have, in many areas, enacted broad enabling legislation not only authorizing but encouraging cooperative intergovernmental arrangements. The practical advantages inherent in the procedure contribute to its popularity. Such service agreements do not alter the autonomy or structure of local governments, but they permit the solution to many service-related problems because service areas can be expanded and services delivered on a broad geographic base often more cheaply and more efficiently. On the other hand, problems that may result from conflicting interests and jurisdictions in metropolitan areas are not necessarily solved; rather they may only be alleviated.

The ACIR-ICMA national survey of nearly six thousand incorporated municipal units reveals that they receive a significant number and a large variety of services from other government units by means of informal and formal agreements.[25] Formal and informal agreements can involve any service, but formal agreements tend to relate more to the supply of water, sewage treatment, and joint facilities, while informal agreements, based on verbal understanding, relate chiefly to mutual aid and maintenance of highways and bridges. Unlike the Lakewood Plan in Los Angeles County, in which municipalities contract for all their services from the county, most agreements involve two localities and a single function, rather than a comprehensive package.

Transfer of Functions

Another cooperative agreement is the transfer of a function from one governmental unit, usually small, to another, usually larger, governmental unit. Transfers of functions are generally permanent and involve a shift of fiscal responsibility, policy, and operational authority. Whereas forty-two states have enacted all or part of a model interlocal contract act, only ten states have general constitutional or legislative authority for the transfer of functions.[26] Forty percent of 3300 responding municipalities indicated that they had either assumed a new function or transferred one or more functions to another level of government.[27] The most common transfers have been from the municipality to the county, but some have gone to areawide special districts, to regional councils, and to the state government. Occasionally, as has happened in New York and California, functional transfers result in decentralization when state programs are shifted to regional or local authorities.

CONCLUSION

Norton Long reports that former U.S. Department of Housing and Urban Development Secretary George Romney once traveled the country criticizing the separation between the "real city" or the metropolitan area and the multiple cities.[28] Romney believed that political integration was logical given the economic interdependence of the metropolitan area. But economic arguments have not proved persuasive against the stronger ties of separate local governments.

We have noted local boundary commissions, increased authorities, Montana's statewide local government study, Minnesota's Twin Cities' Metropolitan Council, Nevada's ill-fated consolidation mandate for Las Vegas and Clark County, and other such examples. Yet these examples are few and the basic position of states has been to adhere to a policy of restricted action in the reorganization of metropolitan regions with respect to altering local units to achieve either centralized or decentralized governments.

There is a multiplicity of local governments in metropolitan areas. In part this reflects the fact that there is a multiplicity of interests which only a similar mutiplicity can respond to. There appears to be no major trend toward governmental centralization or decentralization in metropolitan areas. The states have on the whole acted to further the initiatives of local residents. They have, with few exceptions, not imposed major structural reforms upon their urban areas. Rather, they have instituted procedures that assist localities to function more effectively. In addition, states have vastly increased their fiscal aid to localities. It is to the issue of state-local fiscal relationships that we turn next.

NOTES

1. Bureau of the Census, U.S. Department of Commerce Governmental Organization, vol. 1, no. 1, 1977 Census of Governments (Washington, D.C.: U.S. Government Printing Office, 1978), pp. 12-14.

2. "Introduction," ibid., pp. 1-17.
3. Vincent L. Marando and Robert Thomas, The Forgotten Governments: County Commissioners as Policy Makers (Gainesville: University Presses of Florida, 1977), p. 133.
4. Census of Governments (1972); Advisory Commission on Intergovernmental Relations, Regionalism Revisited: Recent Articles and Local Responses (Washington, D.C.: U.S. Government Printing Office, 1977), p. 29
5. Ibid.
6. According to a report in the July 1978 issue of the National Civic Review, county secession moves appeared throughout California based on charges that the counties have not been responding adequately to the needs of the people, that county seats are too far away, and that a new county could provide services at lower cost.
7. Arthur Maass, ed., Area and Power (Glencoe, Ill.: Free Press, 1959), p. 11.
8. Chester C. Maxey, "An Outline for Municipal Government," National Municipal Review 11 (August 1922): 229-230.
9. These have been discussed in Roscoe C. Martin, Metropolis in Transition (Washington, D.C.: U.S. Housing and Home Finance Agency, 1963); John C. Bollens and Henry J. Schmandt, The Metropolis: Its People, Politics, and Economic Life, 2nd ed. (New York: Harper & Row, 1970); and Vincent Marando and Patricia Florestano, "State Commissions on Local Government: A Mechanism for Reform," State and Local Government Review 9, no. 2 (1977).
10. Thor Swanson, "Local Boundary Adjustments and the Administrative Commission," paper delivered at Conference of the American Society for Public Administration, Chicago, 1975, p. 3.
11. Advisory Commission on Intergovernmental Relations, Trends in Metropolitan America (Washington, D.C.: U.S. Government Printing Office, 1977), table 3, pp. 17-19.
12. Richard L. Forstall, "Changes in Land Area for Larger Cities, 1960-1970," Municipal Yearbook 1972 (Washington, D.C.: ICMA, 1972), p. 25.
13. For example, see the Committee for Economic Development, Reshaping Metropolitan Areas (New York: Committee for Economic Development, 1970).
14. Advisory Commission on Intergovernmental Relations, Substate Regionalism and the Federal System, vol. 3, The Challenge of Local Government Reorganization (Washington, D.C.: U.S. Government Printing Office, 1974), p. 95.

15. Parris N. Glendening, "Metropolitan Dade County: A Test of the Local Government Reform Model," paper delivered at Annual American Political Science Association, Washington, D.C., 1968.
16. Ted Kolderie, "Prepared Statement," Fiscal Relations in the American Federal System, hearing before the subcommittee of the committee on Government Operations, House of Representatives, 94th Congress, July 9-24, 1975, pp. 360-363.
17. George Frederickson, ed., Neighborhood Control in the 1970's (New York: Chandler, 1973); Suzanne Keller, The Urban Neighborhood (New York: Random House, 1968); Milton Kotler, Neighborhood Government (Indianapolis: Bobbs-Merrill, 1969); Henry J. Schmandt, "Municipal Decentralization: An Overview," Public Administration Review 32 (October 1972); Donna E. Shalala, Neighborhood Governance Issues and Proposals (New York: American Jewish Consulate, 1971); Paul Studenski and Paul Mort, Centralized Versus Decentralized Government in Relation to Democracy (New York: Columbia University Press, 1939); Douglas R. Yates, Neighborhood Democracy (Lexington, Mass.: Heath, 1973).
18. James W. Fesler, "Centralization and Decentralization," International Encyclopedia of the Social Sciences (1968), 2:370-377.
19. Howard W. Hallman, "Foreword: Curriculum Essays on Cities, Politics, and Administration in Urban Neighborhoods," Public Administration Review 32 (October 1972):ii.
20. Victor Jones, "Representative Local Government: From Neighborhood to Region," Bulletin of Institute of Government Studies, (Berkeley: University of California, April 1970), p. 2.
21. Robert L. Bish and Vincent Ostrom, Understanding Urban Government: Metropolitan Reform Reconsidered (Washington, D.C.: American Enterprise Institute for Public Policy Research, 1973), p. 2.
22. Swanson, "Local Boundary Adjustments."
23. Advisory Commission on Intergovernmental Relations, Substate Regionalism, 3:141.
24. Advisory Commission on Intergovernmental Relations, "Local Government Modernization," State Legislative Program 2, Report M-93 (Washington, D.C.: U.S. Government Printing Office, November 1975).

25. Joseph F. Zimmerman, "Intergovernmental Service Agreements and Transfer of Functions," in Advisory Commission on Intergovernmental Relations, Substate Regionalism, 3:29-52.
26. Zimmerman, "Intergovernmental Service Agreements."
27. Ibid
28. Norton Long, "Cities without Citizens," paper presented at the American Political Science Association, New York, August 31-September 3, 1978, p. 15.

Chapter 5

FINANCING LOCAL GOVERNMENTS IN METROPOLITAN AREAS

INTRODUCTION

Many urban governments are confronted with fiscal problems. Many urban governments cannot raise sufficient revenues from local sources to meet the service needs that residents require. As metropolitanization has continued, it has fueled the demand that local governments increase services. As the cost of public service delivery goes up, local governments find it more and more difficult to support these expenditures. Although urban services traditionally have been paid for by local revenues, the states and the national government are shouldering larger shares of local expenses. These higher levels of governments have greater taxing capacity and more elastic revenue-raising mechanisms than those of the local level. The localities are increasingly making larger demands upon the revenues of states and the national government.

Although most local governments have need for additional fiscal reserves, such need varies widely among the many different localities in metropolitan areas. This fiscal imbalance arises from the fact that availability of tax resources and expenditure requirements are not the same for all local governments in metropolitan areas. Governmental decentralization leaves some local units with residents requiring high-cost service, such as health care, and relatively limited local resources, while leaving other units with residents requiring few high-cost services and adequate resources. Central cities and older suburbs have higher proportions of the poor, the elderly, and minorities, who pay little in taxes but require large expenditures for costly services such as health care and welfare.

Along with the revenues that are available locally, this chapter examines the types of expenditures that are necessary and most frequent at the local level in metropolitan areas. We look at differences

Revenues: Local Sources / 87

in expenditure capacities and current trends in these among local units. An essential aspect of this discussion is the contrast between metropolitan communities with central cities which can be regarded as "hardship" cases and those local governments which lack severe financial problems. We consider the local government's responsibility for its own local fiscal actions and state awareness and actions directed at the disparities in needs and resources among local units within metropolitan areas. We also examine the state-imposed limitations on local revenue sources and the types of revenue that can be utilized by localities. State aid is an important aspect of this discussion because the amount of state aid as a percentage of local revenues has been increasing. We further look at state constraints and limitations in the form of mandates, state assumption of services, and state-imposed minimum standards upon local governments. Finally, we raise some public policy questions regarding state control, variance in fiscal policy, and citizen preferences for services.

REVENUES: LOCAL SOURCES

Local revenues are derived from a wide variety of taxes and user charges. All states differ in the latitude given localities to raise resources. State and local revenues are derived from a combination of property taxes, general sales and gross receipts taxes, individual income taxes, franchises and user charges, and federal aid. As Fig. 5.1 shows, the property tax is the principle source of state-local revenue, but in proportion to the other sources it has decreased from 53% in 1942 to 36.6% in 1975. Thus, in those years reliance on general sales and gross receipt taxes has increased steadily, from 7.4 to 20.6%, and income tax has increased from 3.2 to 15.4%. Figure 5.2 illustrates how much the amount and diversity of revenues has increased between 1954 and 1974. Total state-local revenues increased from $35.4 billion to $237.9 billion in those twenty years. This represents an increase of 660% as contrasted against a total population increase for the United States of approximately 25% during the same twenty-year period. The most dramatic increases in state-local revenues came from federal aid and state income taxes. By 1974, the sources of revenue that could be relied upon had become much more diversified. This signifies that the diversification of revenue sources is evening out and that the wealth of communities is better able to be tapped. As the total demand for revenues increases, different sources must be relied upon, with states and localities seeking greater federal aid and localities seeking more state aid.

88 / Financing Local Governments

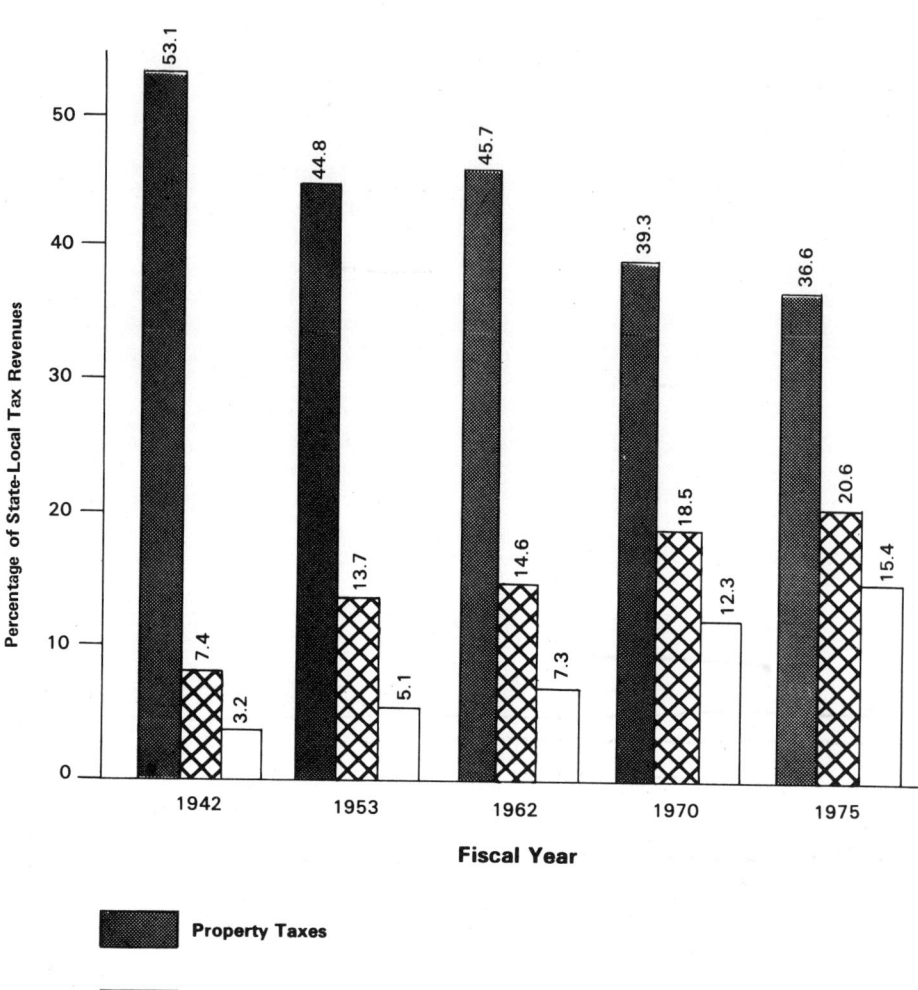

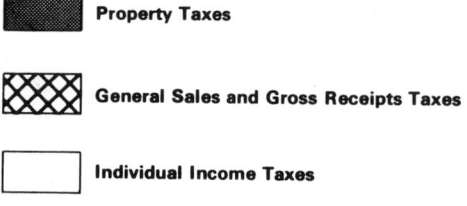

Figure 5.1 Proportions of total state-local tax revenue contributed by the three major sources, selected years 1942-1975. Source: Advisory Commission on Intergovernmental Relations compilation based on U.S. Bureau of the Census data; shown in Improving Urban America: A Challenge to Federalism, M-107, September 1976, p. 50.

1954

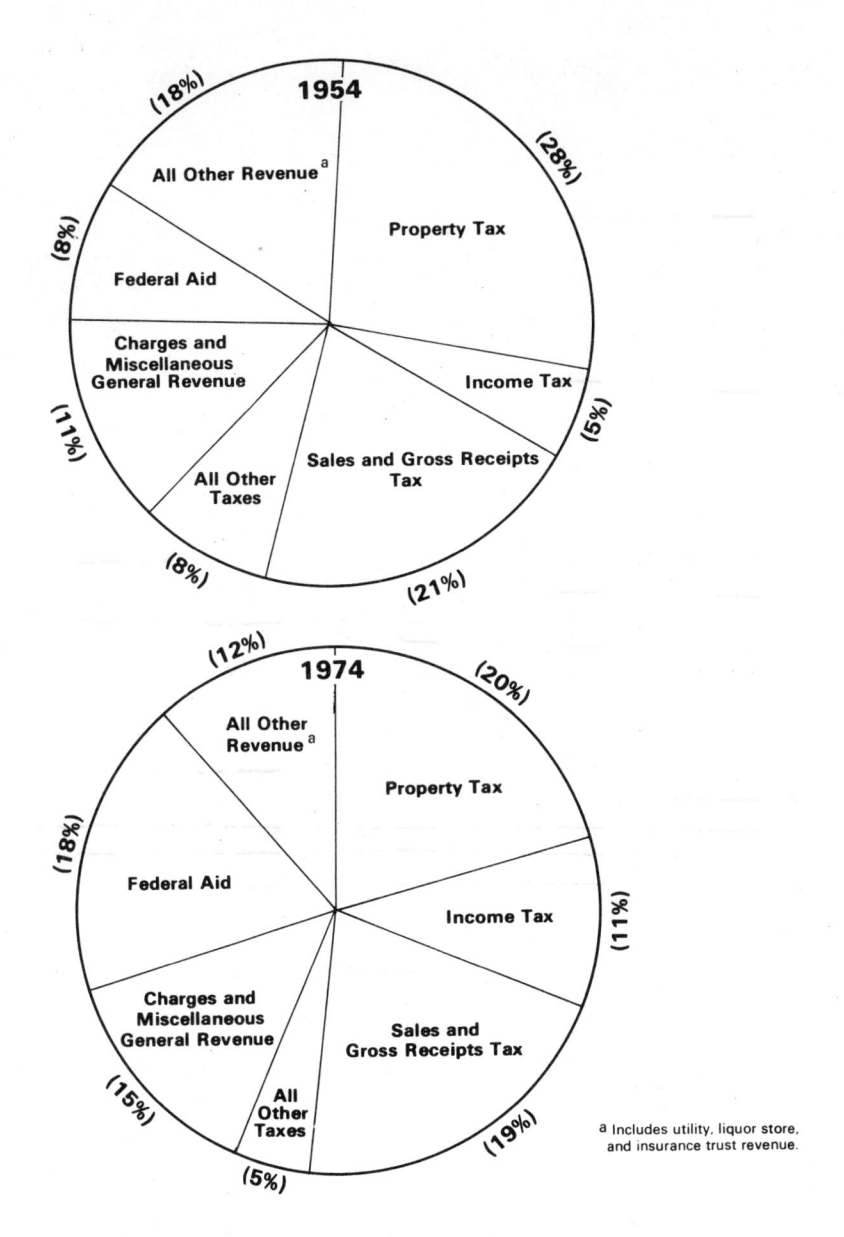

- Property Tax (28%)
- Income Tax (5%)
- Sales and Gross Receipts Tax (21%)
- All Other Taxes (8%)
- Charges and Miscellaneous General Revenue (11%)
- Federal Aid (8%)
- All Other Revenue [a] (18%)

1974

- Property Tax (20%)
- Income Tax (11%)
- Sales and Gross Receipts Tax (19%)
- All Other Taxes (5%)
- Charges and Miscellaneous General Revenue (15%)
- Federal Aid (18%)
- All Other Revenue [a] (12%)

[a] Includes utility, liquor store, and insurance trust revenue.

Figure 5.2 The state and local revenue system becomes more diversified with the relative decline in property taxes and relative increase in state income taxes and federal aid, fiscal years 1954 and 1974.
Source: ACIR compilation based on U.S. Bureau of the Census data; shown in Improving Urban America: A Challenge to Federalism, M-107 September 1976, p. 52.

Property Taxes

The financial backbone for both state and local governments throughout our history has been the general property tax. With the expansion of revenue needs, the states have largely abandoned the property tax to the localities and have substituted other forms for themselves, as can be seen in Table 5.1. Thus, property taxes account for 2% of state taxes, but for 83% of locally raised taxes. The property tax remains the backbone of local revenues because the states and national levels of government have not preempted it. As can be seen in Fig. 5.3, the Northeast, the Midwest, and California utilize the property tax most extensively; the South as a region uses the property tax least. Additionally, although the revenue it produces varies, the property tax is the largest revenue producer subject to local control and administration. The tax is based primarily on property such as real estate and buildings which is immobile and therefore cannot easily be moved to another jurisdiction. Therefore, localities have "access" to taxing property within their jurisdictions.

On the other hand, the property tax is criticized as being regressive, inelastic, oppressive, a poor measure of wealth, and subject

Table 5.1 State and Local Taxes, by Source, 1972-1973 (in Billions of Dollars)

	State taxes		Local taxes	
	Amount	Percentage	Amount	Percentage
All taxes	$68.1	100	$53.0	100
Income	21.0	31	2.4	4
Individual	15.6	23	2.4	4
Corporation	5.4	8	—	—
Property	1.3	2	44.0	83
Sales, gross receipts	37.1[a]	54	4.9	9
General	20.0	29	3.2	6
Selective	17.3	25	1.7	3
All other	8.6	13	1.7	3

[a] Totals do not add due to rounding.
Source: Bureau of the Census, U.S. Department of Commerce, Governmental Finances in 1972-73. Reproduced from National Governor's Conference, States Responsibility to Local Governments: An Action Agenda (Washington, D.C.: U.S. Government Printing Office, October 1975), p. 170.

Revenues: Local Sources / 91

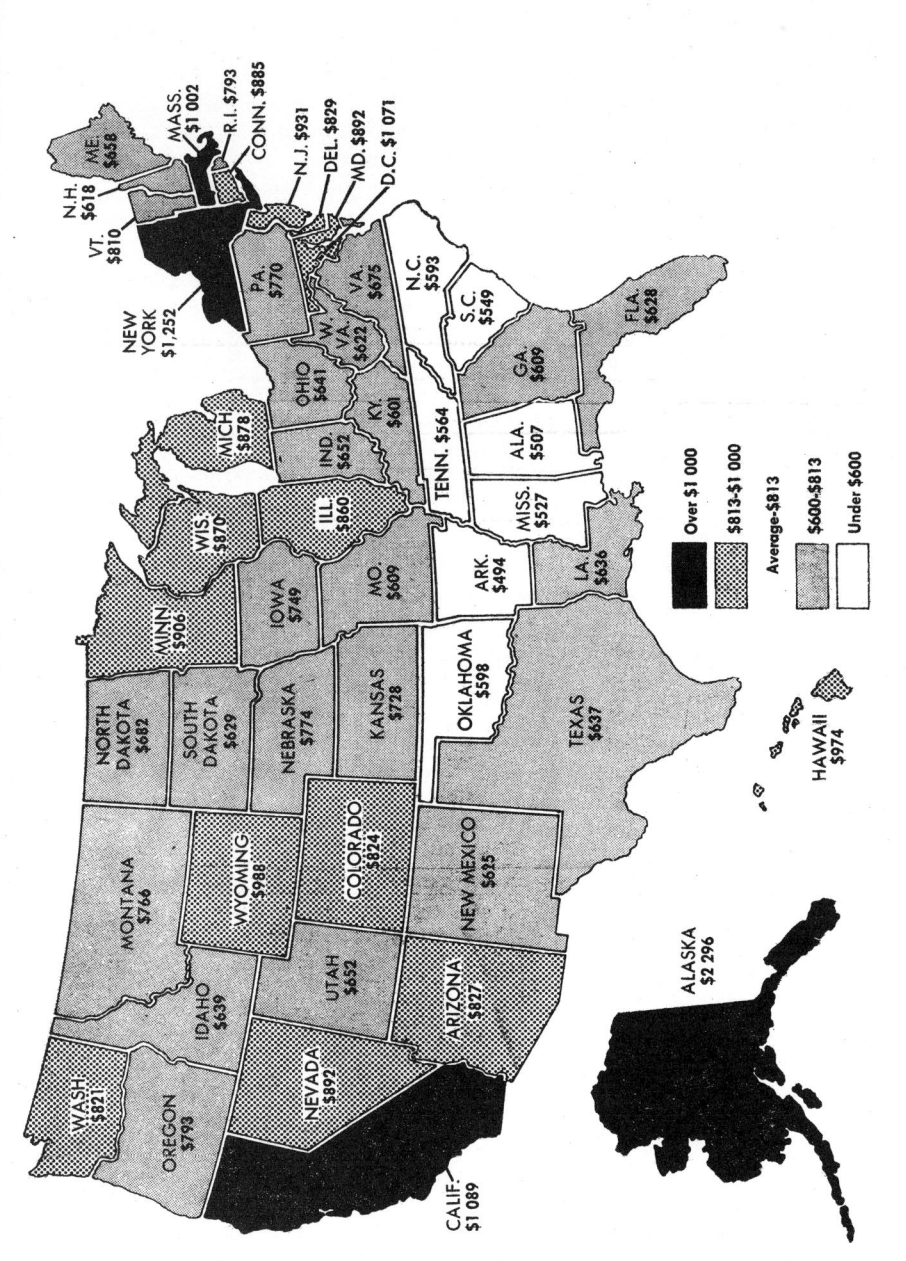

Figure 5.3 State and local per capita tax burden, fiscal year 1976-1977. Source: Commerce Clearing House, Inc. © The Washington Post.

to misuse via improperly and poorly administered assessment practices. No tax has been subjected to more criticism on equity grounds than the property tax. First of all, the exemption process whereby certain groups are exempted from the tax or taxed at a reduced rate is criticized. Properties used for charitable, religious, or educational purposes are almost always exempted on the assumption that they are rendering a public service. Government property is always exempt from taxation by other governments. Additionally, certain states attempt to attract new industry by granting them tax exemptions for a specific period. Often, it is the central city, with the highest proportion of the metropolitan area's poor, that has the most property exempt from taxation. A study by Bahl estimates that $600 billion worth of real estate, or one-third of the U.S. total, is not taxed at all.[1] Such taxes must be made up by those who are not exempt from the property tax.

To begin with, assessors tend to be chosen on the basis of popular election rather than professional training. As a consequence, the values they place on the pieces of property in their jurisdictions as they develop the assessment roles are often somewhat questionable. Assessment roles, therefore, do not necessarily reflect the true value of the property under assessment, and varied assessments result from political pressure. In a study done for the Senate Subcommittee on Intergovernmental Relations, Arthur D. Little, Inc. found not only inequality of property tax levels among neighborhoods, but also that poor-quality housing in blighted neighborhoods was taxed at a substantially higher rate than property in other neighborhoods.[2]

Probably for all of these reasons and others, the local property tax is regarded as the worst tax, the least fair tax, by the American public. In a survey published in 1977, the Advisory Commission on Intergovernmental Relations (ACIR) reported that 33% of their respondents regarded the property tax as least fair, as compared to 29% in 1972.[3] Reluctant to relinquish such a heavily utilized form of revenue but sensitive to citizen feelings, states began in the 1970s to give some relief to property owners. Based upon pioneering programs in Wisconsin, Minnesota, and Vermont, numerous states have developed and supported legislation for some form of property tax relief program. Recently, state property tax reform has attempted to bring actual valuation and assessment practices into closer alignment, to open the assessment process to public scrutiny, to improve the quality of assessors, and to provide relief for homeowners and renters with excessive tax burdens, particularly the elderly and low-income groups.[4]

Nevertheless, such reform may not be sufficient. The action of California voters in June 1978 signaled the eruption of a widespread "taxpayer revolt," long threatened but slow to materialize. In that primary election, Californians voted by a two-to-one margin to limit residential as well as commercial property taxes to 1% of a property's market value. The approved resolution, Proposition 13, specifies the cash value as whatever appeared on the public records in 1976, if the house had not been sold since then; and it limits any tax raise by local governments to 2% per year. The proposition also requires any new statewide taxes to be approved by a two-thirds majority of the legislature. City, county, town, and school administrators estimated that they would lose approximately $7 billion a year. After that successful action, support of similar referenda sprang up in states across the country.

Sales Taxes

State sales taxes, taken together, are the single most lucrative source of income to state governments, making up 54% of their total revenues (see Table 5.1). But local sales taxes, although the largest nonproperty tax producers after the property tax, represents only 9% of local tax revenue. As shown in Table 5.2, sales taxes provided local governments with only $24 per capita compared to $210 per capita from property taxes. In many states a portion of the state sales tax is "shared" with local governments. Critics of the general sales tax consider it to be one of the most regressive taxes, in that the tax burden bears no relation to ability to pay. Supporters argue that the sales tax has a high revenue yield and is simple to administer, and that in a generally affluent society even low-income groups should bear a portion of the costs of government. Critics concede that the degree of regressivity can be modified if the "necessities"—food and medicine, for example—are exempted from the sales tax. Central cities often utilize the local sales tax in an effort to tap the resources of visitors and suburban commuters who own no property within the city but who use its services.

Local sales taxes have become more widespread. As of 1975 they accounted for 13% of total taxes among municipalities and 10% of total counties' taxes.[5] Local sales tax rates vary from 3 to 0.5%, with most municipalities and counties utilizing a 1% rate. Out of 78,218 local governments in the country, 4691 utilize a sales tax. These are usually the larger cities and counties.[6] In sixteen states, the local sales tax is applied in all localities statewide, whereas in twenty-seven states it is authorized only for some jurisdictions, often the largest jurisdictions.[7] Because of this, citizens in metropolitan areas often find that one or a few localities utilize the tax while an equal number do not. This situation becomes even more complicated

94 / Financing Local Governments

Table 5.2 Local Taxes per Capita, by Source, 1972-1973

	All local governments	Cities All cities	1 Million population and over	500,000 to 999,999	Less than 50,000
Total taxes	$253	$140	$316	$195	$75
Income	12	—	—	—	—
Property	210	90	175	113	54
Sales					9
General	15	16	39	23	5
Selective	8	11	27	20	8
All other	9	23	75	39	

Source: Bureau of the Census, U.S. Department of Commerce, City Government Finances, 1972-1973. Reproduced from National Governor's Conference, State Responsibilities to Local Governments: An Action Agenda (Washington, D.C.: U.S. Government Printing Office, October 1975), p. 172.

in interstate metropolitan areas where the sales tax may be used in one state and not the other.

Income Taxes

Income taxes are the second largest revenue producer for the forty-six states which impose this form of taxation, making up 31% of the tax source. At the local level it is still a very infrequently used form of taxation, however, amounting to only 4% of the tax source (see Table 5.1). The first local income tax that is still in existence was imposed in Philadelphia in 1939. Eleven states authorize the 4048 jurisdictions in their boundaries to collect a local income tax. In these cases, localities usually may opt by referendum to impose a local income tax. Cities using the tax range from New York City to villages of several hundred people, but they include the major cities of Detroit, St. Louis, Philadelphia, Pittsburgh, and Baltimore. But because localities fear that such income taxes can cause out-migration of people and industry to the suburbs, they are often reluctant to levy this type of tax.

Other Taxes

User taxes, often referred to as "nuisance" taxes, account for only 3% of state and local taxes, as Table 5.1 shows. User taxes are applied to utility rates, telephone service, parking, and liquor sales. Beyond that, a variety of factors such as location, natural resources, and economic base create different revenue sources for governmental units. Licenses, permits, and charges for current services such as admissions and amusement taxes, property transfers and records, trailer park taxes, and hotel, motel, and occupancy taxes are exampler, as are fines and forfeitures, interest on funds, and liquor sales.

In many states, income, sales, and other taxes are collected by the states instead of the locality, because of their more efficient collection system, and then returned to the locality. Three other sources of revenue for local governments have not yet been mentioned. Borrowing, a mechanism we do not examine, is used to generate revenue, chiefly for long-term capital improvements. State constraints and limitations on taxing and borrowing by localities, long a problem for local governments, is the subject of the next section. Grants-in-aid from both the national and the state governments, which are rapidly becoming major sources of revenue for many localities, will be discussed in subsequent sections.

EXPENDITURES

How do states and localities spend their money? More than 70% of all state-local expenditures is accounted for by four major functions. As of 1976, the largest outlays were for (1) elementary and secondary education, $67 billion; (2) public welfare, $32 billion; (3) highways, $23 billion; and (4) health and hospitals, $20 billion. Criminal justice, another major service, is costing $16 billion.[8] At the state level, the three functions of education, public assistance, and highways account for about 80% of total expenditures. Expenditure proportions vary across states depending upon whether programs are administered directly by the state or through local governments.

At the local level, expenditures vary significantly depending upon the type of unit. As one would expect, independent school districts apply 100% of their expenditures toward education. However, the two major general-purpose governments of municipalities and counties have different expenditure patterns from one another. Figure 5-4, which shows municipal expenditures by function, indicates that utilities and police and fire protection are the two single largest expenditures. Sanitation accounted for $5.8 billion of total municipal

96 / Financing Local Governments

Total Expenditure $71.2 Billion

- Insurance Trust and Liquor Stores Expenditure $2.3 Billion
- Utility Expenditure $12.1 Billion
- Education $7.8 Billion
- Highways $4.3 Billion
- Police and Fire Protection $10.0 Billion
- Sanitation $5.8 Billion
- Public Welfare $4.6 Bil.
- Health and Hospitals $3.4 Billion
- All Other $20.8 Billion*
- General Expenditure $56.8 Billion

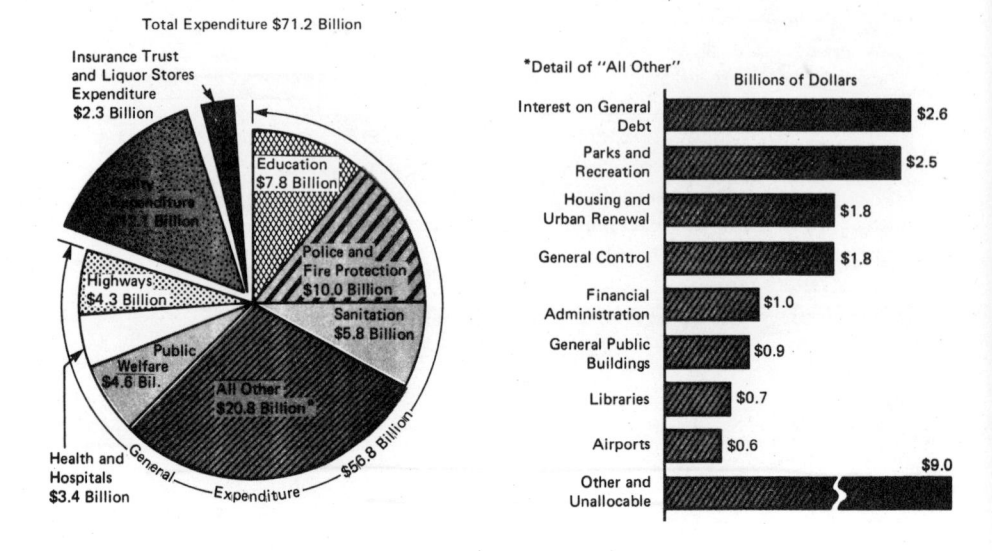

*Detail of "All Other" — Billions of Dollars

Interest on General Debt	$2.6
Parks and Recreation	$2.5
Housing and Urban Renewal	$1.8
General Control	$1.8
Financial Administration	$1.0
General Public Buildings	$0.9
Libraries	$0.7
Airports	$0.6
Other and Unallocable	$9.0

Figure 5.4 Expenditure of municipal governments, by function: 1979-1977. Source: U.S. Department of Commerce, Bureau of the Census, Finances of Municipalities and Township Governments, Vol. 4, Governmental Finances, No. 4, 1977, Census of Governments, p. 9.

expenditures in 1976-1977. Figure 5.5, which shows county expenditures by function, indicates that public welfare is the single largest expenditure at $7.8 billion or 18.8%. To the extent that municipalities and counties operate school systems, education expenditures are a substantial portion of the budget in each type of local government. There is a close correspondence between cities and counties as to how expenditures are allocated by function. Both municipalities and counties expend appreciable sums for health, hospitals, highways, and public welfare.

The size of a local unit and its location inside or outside a metropolitan area are two factors which affect the kind and amount of demand for public services and hence produce variations in expenditure patterns. While two of the three highest expenditures for local governments both inside and outside metropolitan areas are education and health, the second highest expenditure differs according to location, as seen in Figure 5-6. For local governments inside metropolitan areas this

Expenditures / 97

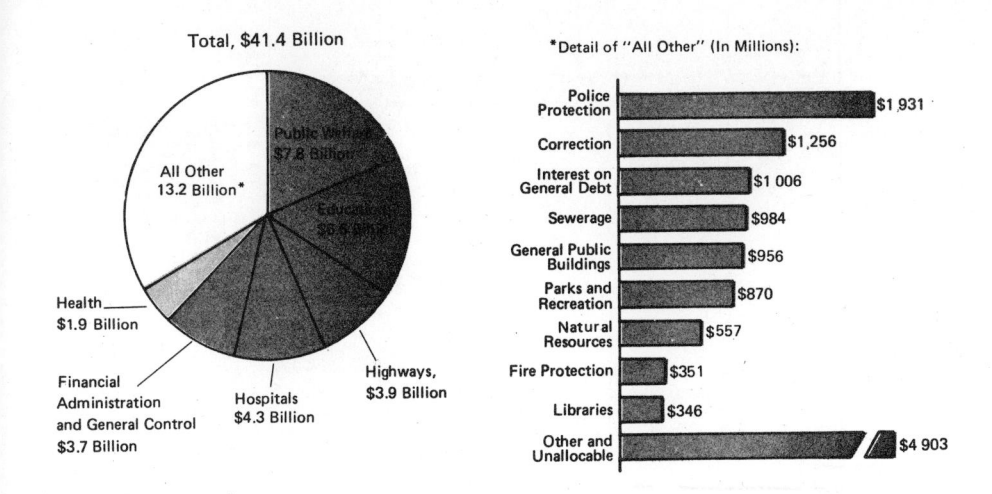

Figure 5.5 General expenditure of county governments, by function: 1976-1977. Source: U.S. Department of Commerce, Bureau of the Census, Finances of County Governments.

expenditure is welfare, while for those outside it it is highways. But in all other areas except highways, local governments inside metropolitan areas spend more per capita than ones outside.

Figure 5.7 shows local government expenditures for services as related to the size of the metropolitan area. Table 5.3, which lists the seventy-two largest SMSAs by region, breaks down expenditures between central cities and areas outside central cities by educational and noneducational services. Virtually all central cities spend more in total than do non-central cities, but educational expenditures are higher in most non-central-city areas than in central cities. Often suburban cities do not support many services apart from education. There are several SMSAs, however, in which central cities not only spend more dollars in total but more total dollars or higher percentages of money for education than non-central-city areas. The reason is to be found in state aid for local governments. If statewide educational aid is based mostly on need, central city aid from the state is high, reflecting state compensation of their depressed status.

Since 1960 the rate of growth of state and local spending has exceeded that of the national government. Several factors explain this

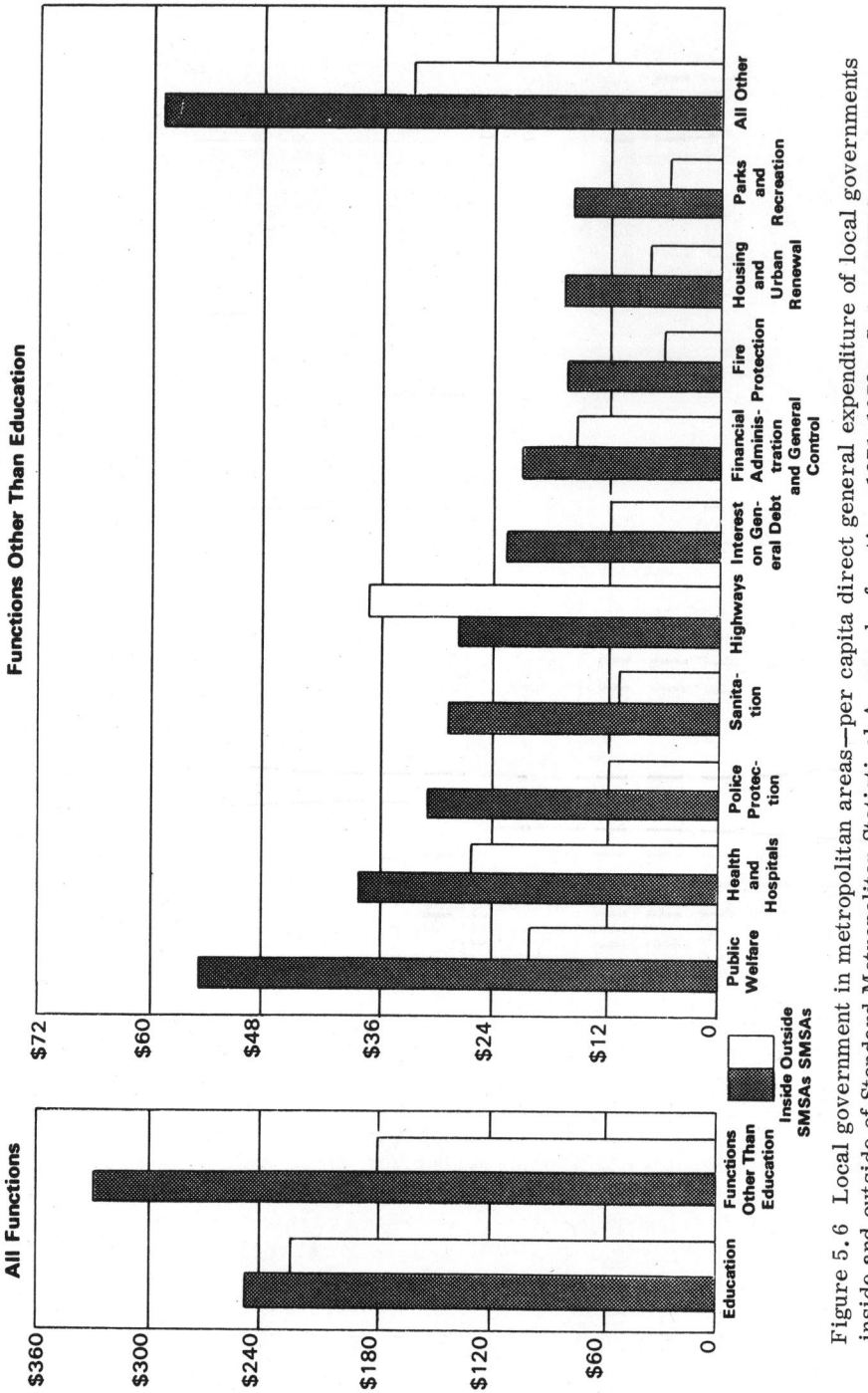

Figure 5.6 Local government in metropolitan areas—per capita direct general expenditure of local governments inside and outside of Standard Metropolitan Statistical Areas, by function, 1971-1972. Source: U.S. Department of Commerce, Social and Economic Statistics Administration, Bureau of the Census data; shown in Improving Urban America: A Challenge to Federalism, M-107, September 1976, p. 71.

Figure 5.7 Per capita direct general expenditure of local governments for selected functions in various size groups of Standard Metropolitan Statistical Areas, 1971-1972. Source: U. S. Department of Commerce, Social and Economic Statistics Administration, Bureau of the Census; shown in Improving Urban America: A Challenge to Federalism, M-107, September 1976, p. 52.

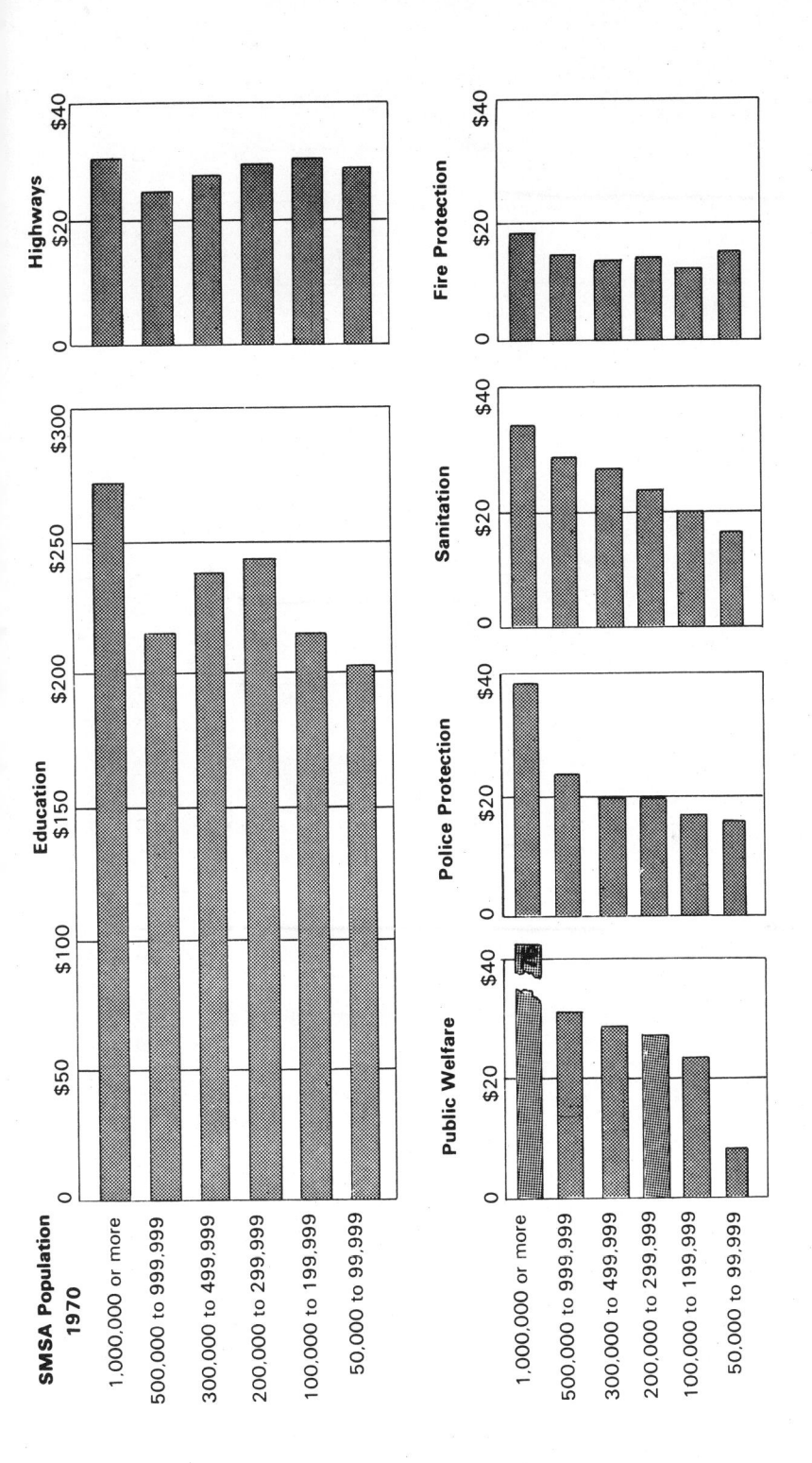

Table 5.3 Per Capita Noneducational and Educational Expenditures, 72 Largest SMSAs, 1970

Region and SMSA	Total expenditures CC	Total expenditures OCC	Educational expenditures CC	Educational expenditures OCC	Noneducational expenditures CC	Noneducational expenditures OCC
Northeast	$ 551	$405	$181	$223	$370	$182
Hartford, Conn.	501	399	208	214	293	185
Wilmington, Del.	679	303	251	210	428	93
Washington, D.C.	1006	425	261	244	745	181
Baltimore, Md.	638	349	222	215	416	134
Boston, Mass.	531	365	139	177	392	188
Springfield, Mass.	393	310	155	167	238	143
Jersey City, N.J.	454	357	128	109	326	248
Newark, N.J.	735	441	216	205	519	236
Paterson-Clifton-Passaic, N.J.	381	418	141	197	240	221
Albany-Schenectady-Troy, N.Y.	473	495	161	289	312	206
Buffalo, N.Y.	528	520	165	261	363	259
New York City, N.Y.	894	644	215	332	679	312
Rochester, N.Y.	699	549	225	325	474	224
Syracuse, N.Y.	561	586	159	318	402	268
Allentown-Bethelem-Easton, Pa.	312	348	138	228	174	120
Harrisburg, Pa.	359	297	204	216	174	120
Philadelphia, Pa.	495	325	174	203	321	122
Pittsburg, Pa.	450	309	154	180	296	
Providence, R.I.	392	265	139	146	253	119
Midwest	480	349	183	200	297	149
Chicago, Ill.	478	346	158	199	320	147
Gary-Hammond-East Chicago, Ind.	465	310	244	184	221	126
Indianapolis, Ind.	355	306	144	194	211	112
Wichita, Kansas	474	360	164	225	310	135
Detroit, Michigan	471	462	177	261	294	201
Flint, Michigan	747	449	289	240	458	209
Grand Rapids, Mich.	434	364	198	186	236	178
Minneapolis-St. Paul, Minn.	540	520	154	234	386	236

Table 5.3 (Continued)

Region and SMSA	Total expenditures CC	Total expenditures OCC	Educational expenditures CC	Educational expenditures OCC	Noneducational expenditures CC	Noneducational expenditures OCC
Midwest (cont.)						
Kansas City, Mo.	$ 485	$347	$169	$194	$316	$153
St. Louis, Mo.	463	292	176	187	287	105
Omaha, Neb.	335	338	135	243	200	95
Akron, Ohio	412	310	148	186	264	124
Cincinnati, Ohio	761	262	343	131	418	131
Cleveland, Ohio	512	368	210	195	302	173
Columbus, Ohio	398	290	133	179	265	111
Dayton, Ohio	456	291	165	171	291	120
Toledo, Ohio	444	294	146	150	298	144
Youngstown-Warren, Ohio	335	236	135	144	200	92
Milwaukee, Wisc.	562	486	183	250	379	236
South	383	270	153	164	230	106
Birmingham, Ala.	334	244	111	153	223	91
Mobile, Ala.	333	188	109	106	224	82
Jacksonville, Fla.	307	0	167	0	140	0
Miami, Fla.	481	387	202	202	279	185
Tampa-St. Petersburg, Fla.	372	288	162	162	210	128
Atlanta, Ga.	554	315	218	191	336	124
Louisville, Ky.	508	302	246	212	282	90
New Orleans, La.	334	325	126	123	208	202
Greensboro-Winston Salem-High Point, N. Car.	433	244	157	150	276	94
Oklahoma City, Okla.	296	264	118	157	178	107
Tulsa, Okla.	306	202	146	121	160	81
Knoxville, Tenn.	372	228	134	157	238	71
Memphis, Tenn.	370	240	135	183	235	57

Key: CC = central cities; OCC = outside central cities.
Source: Advisory Commission on Intergovernmental Relations, City Financial Emergencies: The Intergovernmental Dimension (Washington, D.C.: U.S. Government Printing Office, 1973), p. 133.

rapid growth during recent decades. For one, the age groupings that require heavy public expenditures (e.g., the young and the elderly) increased at higher rates than did the general population. For example, from 1949 to 1969, the population grew by 36%, but the number of public school students rose by 89%. Although the middle years of the 1970s have begun to show a slight decline in the birth rate, the number of elderly persons continues to rise. A second factor that has affected all costs, both public and private, local and national, has been inflation, which hits particularly hard at expenditures for public employees. Third, population increases in metropolitan areas push up these costs because such increases require the initiation of new as well as the expansion of established urban services. And clearly the governmental and other public service needs—be they for public health, transportation, water supplies, or whatever—are more than proportionately greater for groups of people such as are gathered in our metropolitan areas than they are for smaller groups as in our rural areas. Finally, metropolitan area governments must cope with their higher concentrations of the disadvantaged of our society, whose need for public services we acknowledge.[9]

Expenditure patterns have been determined in the past by income available, by population density, by the central-city proportion of that population, by urbanization, and by state and federal aid.[10] Researchers have found that income, population, and government aid generally explain over three-quarters of the variance in local government expenditures. This seems to imply that much of local governmental cost is related to locally based factors beyond easy manipulation by state policymakers. The differences between metropolitan and nonmetropolitan expenditures imply that states may have differing state aid structures for each.

It is impossible to be precise as to future expenditure trends. The strong upward spiral in state and local finances does not show any signs of slackening, especially in metropolitan areas. Some of the underlying factors that have pushed up expenditures are expected to continue doing so in the immediate future. Although the birth rate has declined somewhat, the population continues to grow and will do so for many decades even if the decline in births continues. Demographers have pointed out that the middle years of the 1970s witnessed the first perceptible drop in population in metropolitan areas. This may be a harbinger of future population trends, but once again we see no overall decline in urban areas or in the amount of urbanization. Finally, rising price levels and higher incomes seem to be a fixed pattern in our economy.

To these factors public employee unionism and collective bargaining have added new pressures for increased expenditures. This phenomenon produces sharply rising public salaries, more generous fringe benefits, and larger pensions. The latter, in particular, threaten to overwhelm local governments and were considered a major factor in New York City's fiscal problem. A second new area of stress relates to rising costs associated with energy needs and the costs of operations and services which are energy-intensive. Local governments are finding, for example, that they must budget more for the energy costs of police patrol and highway operations, for fueling transit systems, and for providing heat in public housing.[11] And certainly no one predicts any decrease in energy costs in the near future.

CONTRASTS IN METROPOLITAN COMMUNITIES

In metropolitan areas, financial instability surfaces in different proportions, creating distinct types of financial hardship. Several factors are generally found to contribute to the distress of cities. These include high unemployment; excessive fringe benefits to public employees; high expectations by citizens for extensive low-cost service provision; a high ratio of dependent population to total population; and aging public buildings and infrastructures such as streets, sewers, and water lines.

These conditions of distress can be exacerbated by fiscal gimmickry, such as misassessment of future revenues and sloppy accounting and management, falling bond ratings, inflation, hostile state legislatures, misuse or underuse of employee time, a tax-intolerant citizenry, failure to adapt the tax structures to societal changes, and national economic recessions.

Most of these contributors to fiscal hardship have come together drastically in the central cities of the Northeast and Midwest. Observing them, Stanley distinguishes two types of financial hardship: fiscal crisis and long-term decline.[12] Fiscal crisis is not the annual balance-of-the-budget tug-of-war; it is the city's lack of reserves to meet immediate expenses such as payroll or supplies. Longer-term decline is a general downward slide of a city's economy and social conditions. Comparing half-a-dozen different lists of troubled cities by various economists, Stanley concludes that New York, Buffalo, Detroit, Newark, St. Louis, Boston, Cleveland, and Philadelphia are the most troubled.[13] All of these are in the Northeast or Midwest, a finding also corroborated by a more comprehensive index of central city hardship compiled by Nathan and Adams.[14]

Most of the central cities which are comparatively "better off" are in the South and Far West. Moreover, smaller-size communities in metropolitan areas have not been hit with financial worries to the extent that the larger jurisdictions have. Despite our having long since become an urban nation, 37% of our population still live in communities under 10,000 population. These are places like Clarkson, Washington, with 6875 residents which spent its $179,000 grant of revenue-sharing dollars building an animal shelter and an indoor pistol range; or Port Graham, Alaska, population 122, which received $882,997 in federal assistance to build a community service building.

STATE LIMITATIONS ON LOCAL REVENUES

The states have attempted to regulate local finances by limiting the types of revenues available to localities, the amount of revenues that localities could obtain, and the amount of debt that they could incur.

Local Taxing Powers

States confer on local governments the power to tax. Because most state constitutions say little about nonproperty taxes, localities which have imposed such taxes occasionally have been upheld by the courts on the grounds that they are not forbidden by the Constitution. Generally in the past, however, the availability of nonproperty taxes to local governments has been limited, the only major exception being license taxes. Restrictions on local nonproperty tax powers take three forms.[15] Outright prohibition of local imposition of particular nonproperty taxes is the first kind of restriction. Sometimes such prohibitions, rather than being expressed with reference to a particular local nonproperty tax, are used to safeguard the state's right to preempt certain taxes for its exclusive use. A second restriction is the result of "Dillon's rule" which, as we discussed earlier, denies the right of local self-government. This leads, of course, to the belief that unless there is explicit authorization, there is no power to tax. A third restriction involves situations where authorization of specific nonproperty taxes carries with it limitations, as in maximum tax rates, restriction to geographic or jurisdictional areas, purposes for which the revenue may be used, and requirements regarding the tax base.

Numerous state controls and regulations govern local administration of the property tax. Many of the statutory controls are administrative regulations which relate to reporting requirements, assessing procedures and standards, and use of uniform records. Also, regulatory restrictions are being enacted whereby the state has a part in review or appeal from local assessment procedures. The most common restriction on property taxes is the limitation on the amount of revenue that can be raised—either an overall limitation for all taxing jurisdictions or a specific limitation for each specified type of local government. In most states, limitations are expressed in terms of maximum property tax rates.

Such restrictions have had a damaging effect over the years.[16] They are blamed for the creation of special districts to avoid restrictions, short-term financing to cover operating deficits, much long-term borrowing, numerous pieces of special legislation, impaired ability of local officials to administer effectively, and overcrowding in the courts.

Local Debt

To obtain revenue, governments can tax and they can borrow money. Borrowing is usually for the purposes of construction and other capital outlays which are too costly to finance from current revenues. State constitutions and statutes stipulate very stringently how much localities can borrow, for what purposes borrowing can be done, and the ground rules under which it may be done. Tight state regulation dates back to the 1870s when local governments borrowed heavily and as much as 20% of local government debt was in default. States had to step in with assistance and then they imposed regulations in order to curb continued extravagance. Local government borrowing excesses occurred again during the Depression of the 1930s and in New York in the 1950s and 1970s. Because the states are legally responsible, they have a legitimate concern over the debt status of their localities.

Nevertheless, many of the restrictions are unduly onerous, complicated, and difficult to administer. The most common form of restriction is a limit on the maximum amount of debt that a locality can incur; such a limit is usually tied to the assessable base of the local unit. Other types of restriction are time limits on bond maturity, limits on the rate of interest that a locality may pay, specified purposes for incurring debt, and required citizen referenda on issuance of general obligation bonds.

Because of the problems of working within the numerous rules and regulations, local government officials have developed numerous ways to circumvent state debt regulations. These include the issuance of revenue bonds, payable from earmarked funds generated by a project and not subject to the usual restrictions applied against bonds backed by the full faith and credit of the state; the creation of special districts with separate borrowing limits; the use of special funds and assessments which are not part of the state debt limit; the use of leasing rather than buying; and the use of service contracts or installments.

Tax Lids

In the 1950s, the Council of State Governments produced a lengthy discussion of constitutional restrictions on municipalities including legislative charters, special legislation, municipal home rule, council-manager government, legal rules, and fiscal restraints.[17] A quarter-of-a-century later, constitutional restrictions on local fiscal powers, including local tax limits, local expenditures, and local debt limits, are still the subject of much study.[18] However, new ingredients have been thrown into the controversy. Although we now observe such constraints in terms of efficiency, equity, and economic development, states are introducing novel forms of limits and restrictions that the Council of State Governments did not have to worry about earlier.

In 1976, the ACIR examined state tax and expenditure lids on local government and found that since 1970, fourteen states have enacted some form of new control on local taxing and spending powers. This upsurge in state efforts to control local taxing and spending powers is attributed to public demand for property tax relief, to state efforts to control the growth in school spending, and to a belief on the part of state legislators that local officials need state-imposed restrictions to counter pressures for additional spending.[19]

STATE AID

Types of State Aid

State aid to localities takes several forms. States can increase revenue-raising capacity directly at the local level by authorizing a variety of taxes, or states can broaden local access to borrowing as discussed above. Additionally, the state can itself assume the costs and responsibilities of specified functions, which frees local revenues for other purposes. Also, the state can give tax support to local government through credits and deductions, often in the form of piggybacking or sharing. Finally, the state can give grants-in-aid to the localities either for general fiscal relief or for specific programs.

Tax support to local governments in the form of credits and deductions involves the reduction in state taxes owed because of local taxes paid. This in turn provides an incentive to local governments to raise taxes because the state government will share the increased tax burden. Piggybacking is the mechanism which allows local governments to tie their tax revenues to those of the states. The most common use is with the general sales tax, but some states allow counties to piggyback on the state income tax. In six states, a piggyback tax may be utilized with excise taxes, normally on cigarettes or gasoline.

State grants-in-aid are for categorical programs or of a general revenue-sharing type. The most striking fact about state aid is its growth during this century. Between 1902 and 1975, state financial assistance to local governments rose from $52 million to $52 billion, an increase of a factor of 1000, with the greatest proportion of the increase taking place during the past quarter-century.[20] State aid has also enlarged spectacularly as a proportion of total local revenue: from 6.1% in 1902 to 33.9% in 1974.[21] Even more noteworthy, state intergovernmental aid as a proportion of local general revenue from own sources equaled 62% in 1975, as shown in Table 5.4. State payments to local government totaled $45.6 billion in 1974. Figure 5.8 shows a breakdown by type of local government: $21 billion for school districts, $10.6 billion for counties, and $9.1 billion for municipalities.

Table 5.4 State Intergovernmental Expenditures—U.S. Total, 1975

Category	Expenditure ($ million)	Composition of state aid	Per capita state aid to localities
General	$138,304.0	—	—
Intergovernmental	51,978.3	100%	—
Intergovernmental as % of total state general	—	37.6	—
Intergovernmental			
Education	31,110.2	59.0	$146.47
Highways	3,225.0	6.2	15.18
Welfare	8,101.5	15.6	38.14
General	5,129.3	9.8	—
All other	4,412.4	8.5	20.85
Intergovernmental as % of local general revenue from own sources	—	62.1	—

Source: Adapted from Advisory Commission on Intergovernmental Relations, The States and Intergovernmental Aids (Washington, D.C.: U.S. Government Printing Office, February 1977), tables 1 and 6, and ACIR, Significant Features of Fiscal Federalism, 1976-1977 Edition, vol. 2, Revenue and Debt (Washington, D.C.: U.S. Government Printing Office, March 1977), tables 42 and 43.

108 / Financing Local Governments

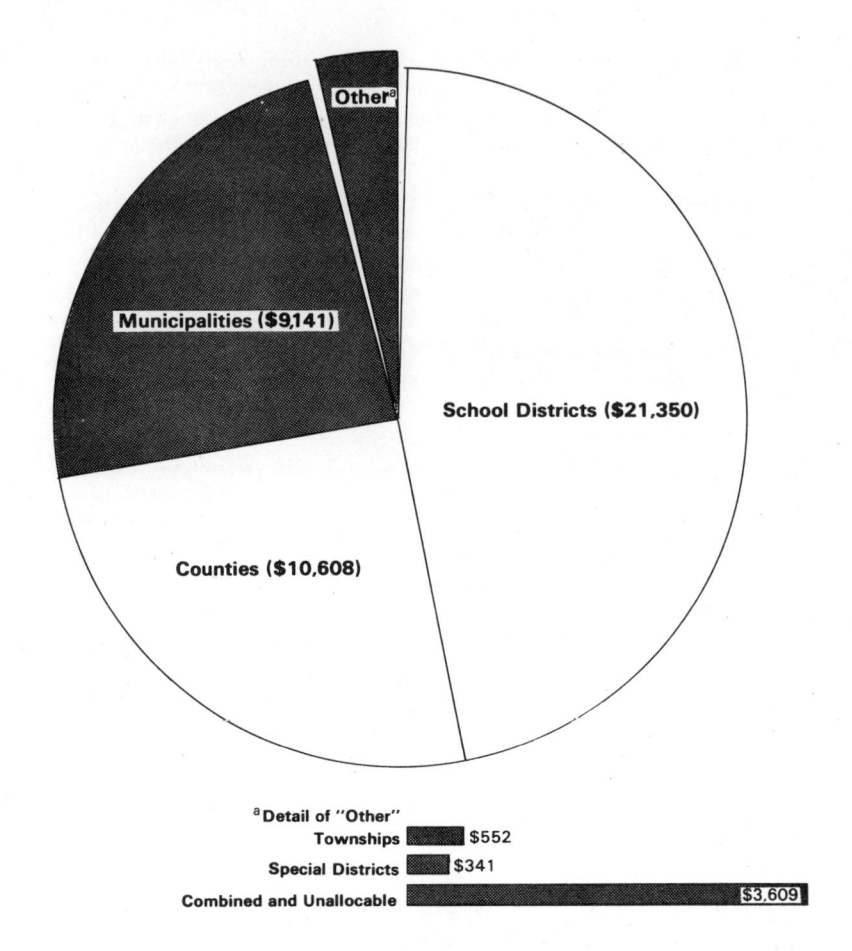

School Districts ($21,350)
Municipalities ($9,141)
Counties ($10,608)
Other[a]

[a] Detail of "Other"
Townships $552
Special Districts $341
Combined and Unallocable $3,609

Figure 5.8 State payments to local governments, by function, 1974—$45.6 billion (in millions of dollars). Source: U.S. Department of Commerce, Social, and Economic Statistics Administration, Bureau of the Census, updated by ACIR staff; shown in Improving Urban America: A Challenge to Federalism, M-107, September 1976, p. 66.

The overwhelming majority of state aid dollars to localities is designated for a specific activity rather than for general purposes. Formula-based grants accounted for $36 billion of $36.8 billion in 1972, and 1804 of the 2121 grants, or 85%.[22] As these figures show, state aid is distributed principally in the four largest functional areas of education, highways, welfare, and health. Nevertheless, there has been some growth in programs of general assistance to local governments. As of 1972, there were 209 state revenue-sharing programs compared with 141 in 1957.[23]

Another dimension of state aid to localities, and one that is very important to local governments in metropolitan areas, is state government support for functions and programs generally considered to be urban. Urban and municipal state aid programs, including 24 municipal programs plus mass transit, airports, planning, and the Older Americans' Program, totaled $900 billion in 1972, as shown in Table 5.5. There were 223 programs in the 24 individual program areas of municipal functions. But aside from police and libraries funds, only a handful of states provide assistance for other urban programs; this assistance is concentrated in ten states which account for over three-fourths of the aid provided.[24] The results are similar with regard to urban programs, which includes 24 defined as municipal, plus mass transit, airports, planning, and the Older Americans' Program. These four functional areas had 69 state programs in 1972, with the largest single program area being aid to mass transit. The encouraging factor in state aid to urban and municipal functions is that though these programs are small, there is a continuing increase both in the number of programs and in the amount of state support. But state response is now widespread.

With regard to distressed areas, there is as yet little attempt to target state aid or to aim at equalization measures. Generally, the state aid system is based on measures that are not equalizing, based on formula principles. Equalization measures are of prime importance only in public education and in some programs of general local government support. Mushkin and Biederman note that "state aid per capita is not directed toward either poor governments or poor people."[25] Studying the existing per capita distribution patterns of state aid, they found that relative degrees of social welfare needs did not explain such patterns. Additionally, they say that "among urban areas particularly, relatively little of that variance was accounted for by differences in urban concentration and degrees of proverty among the respective governments and people."[26] In attempting to measure the amount of state aid oriented toward urban programs, the ACIR reports a figure of 2.5%, while noting that roughly 6 to 7% of all federal aid is targeted toward urban citizen needs.[27]

State Assumption of Services

States can financially aid localities by assuming costs and responsibility for certain functions at the state level. As long ago as the turn

Table 5.5 State Aid for Municipal–Urban Programs, 1972

| Program | No. of states | No. of programs | Source of funds ||| Amount ($ thousand) |
			State	Federal	State and federal	
Fire protection	8	9	9			$ 16,367
Police protection	7	7	7			49,493
Police and/or firemen pensions	16	20	20			41,469
Sewer construction	6	6	5		1	90,742
Sewage treatment	9	9	9			96,868
Water and sewer facilities	8	9	9			25,000
Water pollution control	7	7	4		3	113,456
Water supply	3	3	2		1	55,226
Animal control	2	2	2			104
Parks and recreation	9	10	9		2	10,881
Zoning						
Code enforcement	3	4	4			15,628
Subdivision control						
Refuse collection						
Public housing	8	13	12		1	93,427
Urban renewal	4	5	3		2	7,497
Libraries	40	43	9	12	22	90,190
Municipal civic centers	1	1	1			31

Community development						
Special urban aid	1	1	1			7,150
Day care facilities	1	1	1			808
Municipal aid	1	1	1			24,468
Model cities	2	2	1	1		2,618
Relocation assistance	1	1	1			426
Total, municipal		154	109	13	32	$741,877
Mass transit	7	8	6	1	1	116,363
Airports	32	34	15	7	12	33,212
Planning	17	17	6	2	9	12,453
Older Americans	10	10		10		1,900
Total, urban		69	27	20	22	$163,928
Total, municipal and urban		223	136	33	54	$905,805

Source: Bureau of the Census, U.S. Department of Commerce, Census of Governments, 1972, vol. 6, no. 3, State Payments to Local Governments (Washington, D.C.: U.S. Government Printing Office, 1974). Reproduced from Advisory Commission on Intergovernmental Relations, The States and Intergovernmental Aids (Washington, D.C.: U.S. Government Printing Office, February 1977), p. 33.

112 / Financing Local Governments

of the century, examples can be found of state assumption of responsibility for one or more functions in metropolitan areas. Prior to 1900, Massachusetts created three state-controlled public authorities, the Metropolitan Sewage Commission, the Metropolitan Parks Commission, and the Metropolitan Water Commission. Until the last decade or so, however, few other states followed this approach.

The functions most often shifted to the state are public health, public welfare, municipal courts, pollution abatement, property tax assessment standards, building codes, land-use regulations, including coastal zones and wetlands, and regulation of surface mining.[28] States have also picked up delivery of social services, building and safety inspections, environmental protection, and administrative and legal functions.

Nevertheless, some observers believe that states have been unwilling to assume more urban functional responsibilities.[29] Only a few states have moved into those areas of expenditures responsibility that primarily benefit urban areas (health, hospitals, and corrections). Callahan and Bosek note that states generally have expanded their revenue-raising capabilities more rapidly than their direct expenditure responsibilities.[30] During the fourteen years from 1958 to 1972 the state proportion of state-local expenditure responsibility increased from 35 to 37% while the state share of state-local revenue raising responsibilities increased from 49 to 55%.[31] Further, the data indicate that most states with major expenditure responsibilities in 1957 continued to maintain them as of 1967, while states that exhibited relatively few assumed responsibilities in 1957 also showed few assumptions of responsibility by 1967.

STATE FISCAL DECISIONS AND FUTURE DIRECTIONS

States have made substantial efforts in assisting local governments and service delivery. The state proportion of state-local finances increased significantly during the last two decades. Approximately 25% of all municipal and county revenues comes from the state. However, these revenues are distributed to all local governments, without much, if any, emphasis on the special problems of metropolitan areas and of their distressed portions in particular. Though states have occasionally given aid to their largest or most distressed cities, as in the case of New York, they have not as yet drawn up any specifically metropolitan fiscal strategies. Instead, some ad hoc attacks have been made here and there upon such metropolitan problems as the fiscal disparities among localities. Thus Minnesota adopted a tax-sharing policy for the Minneapolis-St. Paul area, which is overseen by the area's Metropolitan Council. In this tax-sharing plan, all local governments share in any of the new property tax wealth brought into the area. The locality in which a property-enhancing facility is located (e.g., a factory or shopping center) would receive 60% of the property tax and the remaining 40% is distributed among all the other local governments according to population and fiscal need.

In a survey reported in the National Civic Review, urban politicians bemoaned their governments' indigence.[32] Mayors of large cities complained that the states were failing in their responsibilities and that state legislators seemed to assume that urban problems were caused by profligate city governments, which led states to act in a restraining fashion. Those surveyed cited three major areas in which state policies act against cities—tax structure, housing, and mass transit. First, the tax structure in most states does not permit the city to place more emphasis on income taxes. Second, little new housing for moderate- and low-income families has been built. Third, only small portions of state transportation funds go to mass transit. Atlanta, Georgia is a case in point, despite the area's reputation for maintaining good regional intergovernmental relationships. Two of the metropolitan area's counties refused to join in a regional sales tax to support a regional mass transit system, even though their residents were to be future commuters on the system. What was the state legislature's response? It placed representatives from the two holdout counties on the transportation governing board, despite their intransigence, and it did not reallocate state resource assistance for mass transit. This is a far cry from the political and legal pressure the state could have brought to bear on the two recalcitrant counties to gain their inclusion in the sales tax and to insure that the whole metropolitan area population gained access to the system.

The current effectiveness of state governments in helping to resolve fiscal difficulties in urban and metropolitan areas has been woefully poor according to Mushkin and Biederman.[33] A systematic pattern of state action or state involvement in local finances has yet to emerge. But at least the state government role is steadily expanding as a percentage of state-local general expenditure from own funds, from 46.4% in 1953 to 55.5% in 1976.[34]

In summary, the crucial question is whether local government, especially in metropolitan areas, should be given more fiscal responsibility or states should use a "get tough" policy rather than dissolve authority and tighten their control. The answer to this, as to any complex problem, cannot be simple and direct, black or white. States across the board need, first of all, to develop a coherent fiscal policy for their metropolitan and urban areas, recognizing that density of population and proliferation of governments create problems less likely

114 / Financing Local Governments

to be found in rural or small-town areas. At the same time, state control must be balanced with fairness. It is nothing less than outrageous for the state to mandate services that must be delivered by local governments unless there is assurance that the locality can afford such activity. Several municipalities in Maryland have considered disincorporation because they believe that they could not afford to perform the level of services required by the state's General Assembly.

A last word should be said about home rule and the fervent lip service we give to local self-governance. Kincaid has stated that given a choice between the traditional plea for home rule and financial solvency, local officials choose to go with the latter.[35] Many local communities lack the property or income tax base to sustain themselves without outside aid. In an era of complex and interdependent intergovernmental relationships, financially healthy state governments, and financially struggling local governments, perhaps home rule is an "idea whose time may have come and gone."[36] Norton Long has suggested that, in regard to popular governance, we have become a nation of consumers rather than citizens.[37] He suggests that citizens do not care whether services are financed and delivered by the local, the regional, or the state government as long as they are properly delivered. Keeping these changing trends in mind, we believe that responsibility for the fiscal health and well-being of local governments, particularly in the metropolitan areas, rests squarely on the shoulders of state governments.

NOTES

1. Roy W. Bahl, Metropolitan City Expenditure: A Comparative Analysis (Lexington: University of Kentucky Press, 1966).
2. Arthur D. Little, Inc., A Study of Property Taxes and Urban Blight, Report to the U.S. Department of HUD, July 1973, published by the Subcommittee on Intergovernmental Relations of the Stnate Committee on Government Operations.
3. Advisory Commission on Intergovernmental Relations (hereafter ACIR), Significant Features of Fiscal Federalism, 1978-79 (Washington, D.C.: U.S. Government Printing Office, 1979), p. 63.
4. ACIR, Improving Urban America: A Challenge to Federalism (Washington, D.C.: U.S. Government Printing Office, 1976).
5. See ACIR, Significant Features of Fiscal Federalism, 1976-1977 ed., vol. 2, Revenue and Debt (Washington, D.C.: U.S. Government Printing Office, March 1977), table 14, p. 27.

6. Ibid., table 101, pp. 186-87.
7. ACIR, The States and Intergovernmental Aids (Washington, D.C.: U.S. Government Printing Office, July 1977), p. 2.
8. See ACIR, Significant Features of Fiscal Federalism, 1976-77 ed. Vol. 3, Expenditures (Washington, D.C.: U.S. Government Printing Office, November 1977), table 2, pp. 6, 7.
9. For a detailed account see National Commission on Urban Problems, Building the American City, Report to the Congress and the President of the U.S. (Washington, D.C.: U.S. Government Printing Office, 1968), pp. 355-61.
10. See Seymour Sacks and Robert Harris, "The Determinants of State and Local Government Expenditures and Intergovernmental Flows of Funds," National Tax Journal 17 (March 1963): 75-87; Alan Campbell and Seymour Sacks, Metropolitan America: Fiscal Patterns and Governmental System (The Free Press, 1967); Solomon Fabricant, The Trends of Governmental Activity in the United States Since 1900 (New York: National Bureau of Economic Research, 1952); Roy W. Bahl and Robert J. Saunders, "Determinants of Change in State and Local Government Expenditure," National Tax Journal 18 (March 1965): 50-57; Harvey E. Brazier, City Expenditures in the United States (New York: National Bureau of Economic Research, 1959); Roy W. Bahl, Metropolitan City Expenditures: A Comparative Analysis (Lexington: University of Kentucky Press, 1969).
11. John R. Coleman, "Local Government Viability: Do the Data Speak?" paper presented at the American Society for Public Administration Conference, Chicago, April 2, 1975.
12. David T. Stanley, Cities in Trouble (Columbus, Ohio: Academy for Contemporary Problems, 1976), p. 1.
13. Ibid., p. 5.
14. Richard P. Nathan and Charles Adams, "Understanding Central City Hardships," Political Science Quarterly 91, no. 1 (1976): 50.
15. ACIR, State Constitutional and Statutory Restrictions on Local Taxing Powers (Washington, D.C.: U.S. Government Printing Office, 1962), pp. 79-85.
16. Ibid., and ACIR, Improving Urban America.
17. Council of State Governments, Drafting Committee of State Officials, Suggested State Legislation, 1956 (Chicago, 1955).
18. See, for example, Frank P. Grad, "The State's Capacity to Respond to Urban Problems: The State Constitution," in The States and the Urban Crisis, ed. Alan K. Campbell (Englewood Cliffs, N.J.: Prentics-Hall, 1970).

19. John Shannon and L. Richard Gabler, "Tax Lids and Expenditure Mandates: The Case for Fiscal Fair Play," Intergovernmental Perspectives 3, no. 3 (1977):7-12.
20. ACIR, The States and Intergovernmental Aids, p. 7, and Shannon and Gabler, "Tax Lids and Expenditure Mandates."
21. ACIR, The States and Intergovernmental Aids, p. 7.
22. Ibid., p. 7.
23. Ibid., p. 13.
24. Ibid, pp. 16-17.
25. Selma Mushkin and Kenneth R. Biederman, "Defining Tax and Revenue Relations," in National Governors' Conference, States' Responsibilities to Local Governments (Washington, D.C., 1975).
26. Ibid., p. 168.
27. ACIR, The States and Intergovernmental Aids, p. 32.
28. See ACIR, Pragmatic Federalism: The Reassignment of Functional Responsibility (Washington, D.C.: U.S. Government Printing Office, July 1976).
29. Alan Campbell and Roy Bahl, "The Implications of Local Government Reform: Efficiency, Equity, and Administrative Dimensions, in State and Local Government, ed. Alan K. Campbell and Roy W. Bahl (New York: Free Press, 1976), pp. 185-204.
30. John J. Callahan and Ruth M. Bosek, "State Assumption of Urban Responsibilities: Exception to the Rule or Wave of the Future," in Campbell and Bahl, eds., State and Local Government, pp. 79-91.
31. Ibid.
32. "Cities v. States on Finances," National Civic Review 65, no. 10 (1976):358-59.
33. Mushkin and Biederman, "Defining Tax and Revenue Relations," p. 153.
34. ACIR, The States and Intergovernmental Aids, p. 2.
35. Diane Kincaid, "The Arkansas Plan: Coon Dogs or Community Service?" Publius 8, no. 1 (1978).
36. Daniel J. Elazar, "State-Local Relations: Reviving Old Theory for New Practice," in Partnership within the States: Local Self Government in the Federal System, ed. Stephanie Cole (Urbana: University of Illinois, Philadelphia: Temple University, 1976).
37. Norton Long, "The Three Citizenships," Publius 6, no. 2 (1976): 13-32.

Chapter 6

STATE LAND-USE POLICY

INTRODUCTION

Control over land-use policy is a key lever for influencing the extent and direction of development in urban areas. Urban growth and, for that matter, decline occur in territorial terms. Generally, central cities are losing population, industry, and commercial activities in comparison to suburbia, while the fringe areas are the location for most urban growth that is taking place in America's urban areas. Nevertheless, cities are in various stages of revitalization. This revitalization, invovling the use or reuse of vacant or abandoned sites, is in large measure tied to land-use controls.

Currently there is no single comprehensive organization in metropolitan areas which has policy control to determine how land is to be used. Every metropolitan area has a planning agency, but these agencies do not have the authority to determine land use by means of zoning land or the power to enforce building code regulations. In metropolitan areas, the number of governments that have authority to shape land use and thus influence urban development are many. Land-use power has come to rest with local governments through a process of de facto delegation of state authority. Thus each city, suburb, and, in many instances, county has the power to control land use within its jurisdiction. The resulting authority over land use therefore resides with many local jurisdictions, and resultant land-use policies often are pursued in wholly uncoordinated piecemeal fashion.

The problem of uncoordinated land-use policy is particularly critical in metropolitan areas. As described in previous chapters, local jurisdictions in metropolitan areas are highly specialized and highly interdependent. Industrial, commercial, and residential areas are interrelated, yet land-use development for these functions is often under the control of different local jurisdictions within metropolitan

118 / State Land-Use Policy

areas. Some local jurisdictions, primarily suburban areas, are predominantly residential. Many of these, moreover, are built exclusively for middle- and upper-income residents. Lower-income persons in many urban areas cannot find affordable residences near places of expanding employment opportunities, particularly in suburban areas. Externalities, or spillovers, among local jurisdictions are many. These spillovers may be negative or positive. That is, a local jurisdiction may impose traffic, pollution, and social costs upon neighboring jurisdictions through land-use decisions. By contrast, the residents of some jurisdictions may benefit from the facilities of a neighboring jurisdiction when they can use the other's parks, zoos, and recreational facilities.

Local government land-use policies are pursued in terms of what is "rational" for the local government, i.e., what contributes to the local economy and does not detract from the local environment. Thus local governments want to increase their tax bases by attracting high-income residents and clean industries. Yet what is "rational" for a local government is not always rational for the entire metropolitan area. Other industries, low-income persons, sewage treatment plants, and landfills have to be located somewhere within all metropolitan areas. In every metropolitan area tensions therefore exist between local and metropolitan interests.

The reconciliation of local and metropolitan interests needs to be addressed by a governmental organization with the appropriate territorial scope and authority to determine land-use policy. We argue that if such an organization is to exist, it must be at the state level where the issue of how land is to be used can be decided across the territory of the state. Until very recently, state government has played a very passive role in shaping land-use policy for urban areas. In effect, states had abdicated their authority over land use, but currently they are attempting to reexert their influence in this critical area, and this is a critical urban issue of the 1980s.

Which level of government is to be in control of land use and what values are to be promoted by it are questions that will affect a multitude of activities in urban areas. Land use influences such matters as economic development, environmental protection, transportation, housing practices, and the very makeup and distribution of populations over the urban landscape. This complex of interrelated issues, of which land use is a cornerstone, represents a challenge to state land-use policy development. Urban change is inevitable, whether or not there is a state land-use policy to guide it. Urban change will be influenced by private and public sector decisions. The issue we explore here is what role the state can play in balancing local and metropolitan needs against available land resources.

There are many paradoxes involved in developing a state land-use policy. To protect the environment may mean that economic development is to be limited. The need for additional housing in urban areas, especially for low-income families, often conflicts with the purported desire of middle- and upper-income families to preserve the character of their communities and the value of their homes. The demand for more extensive highways conflicts with the need to meet increasing energy shortages and costs.

Land-use policy is a powerful tool precisely because its exercise influences the resolution of many vested interests and because certain restrictions must be placed upon land use. Local governments clearly do not have the territorial scope or authority to pursue land-use policy for entire areas affected by urbanization. Local governments represent their residents and pursue policies accordingly. At the other extreme of the federal continuum, national government does not have a land-use policy, nor does it appear that it will develop one in the foreseeable future. The failure of Congress to pass a national land-use law in 1974 exemplifies this. The power necessary to develop such a land-use policy does not exist at the national level in part because the states have resisted the formulation of such a policy. In addition, the states are currently reasserting their authority over land-use policy and are resisting federal infringement in this area. The critical questions are what restrictions are to be placed upon land use and what policies will states utilize in affecting urban areas.

STATE LAND USE: THE ISSUES AND INTERESTS

There are two fundamental concerns in the development of an authoritative state land-use policy.[1] First, there is a need to strike a workable and equitable balance between private and public interests. The basic tension in land use is between the rights of individuals to make free choices about the use of their property and the concern of society that those choices do not adversely affect the larger public good. The public interest has expanded over recent decades from one including only health and safety concerns to the public's interest in environmental quality, cultural and aesthetic values, and social and economic needs. The problem of striking a balance among the various interests has become a more complicated intergovernmental task.

As land-use conflicts sharpen, there is a continuous need to reevaluate at which point public constraints upon free personal choice represents a "taking" of property which requires compensation, and there is currently much debate on this. The Fifth Amendment of the Constitution forbids that "private property be taken for public use without just compensation." The controversy over the "taking" issue centers around the point at which the amount of government regulation of the use of private land has become so excessive that it is tantamount to taking away that land without compensation. This "taking issue" will therefore clearly constitute a basic consideration in the development of state land-use policy.

The second basic issue involves the authority of states over local governments in the area of land use. Under test is the point of balance between the interests of a local jurisdiction and the interests of the entire metropolitan area. The very notion of what determines the public interest depends upon whether the point of reference is the locality or the entire metropolis. The interests of local land-use policy may, as indicated above, be at odds with the broader interests of the metropolitan area. Economically distressed central cities clearly have land-use interests very different from affluent suburbs. It is within the state context of authority that these various public interests are undergoing reassessment and reformed land-use policies are emerging.

STATES' REENTRY INTO LAND-USE POLICY

One of the most significant changes in intergovernmental relations over the last several decades has been the reassertion by state governments of the authority to zone land for particular uses, an authority that has hitherto been exercised by local governments.[2] As all local powers flow from state authority, so does the power to determine land use. Until recent decades, state government had little interest in or need to control the use of land. The use of land was considered a local matter to be decided by local political processes. The extent of land-use power was defined by local interests petitioning state and federal courts.[3] Once states delegated land-use authority to localities it was local governments which had the initiative in determining the scope of power over land use.

The scope of local land-use authority was shaped over many decades, primarily through challenges by plaintiffs within the judicial process. State legislatures maintained a passive attitude toward land use, and only in the last two decades have they reasserted authority in this area. As Richard F. Babcock and Fred P. Bosselman indicate, judicial action is a heavy tool with which to fix the intricate clockwork of the land-use controls system.[4] The main point stressed here is that the legal determination of land use through the courts was in reference only to local government land-use regulations and not to state regulation. Before moving on to state land-use policy, we must review the former scope of land-use regulations delegated to localities.

States' Reentry into Land-Use Policy / 121

The legal history is long, with many court cases having an impact on the scope of municipal land-use regulation. Among the many court cases, two in particular stand out as having sustained impact upon land use. The first case is the celebrated Euclid case decided by the United States Supreme Court in 1926.[5] The Ambler Realty Company accused the Village of Euclid, Ohio of overstepping its authority by "taking" property, which is proscribed by the due-process clause of the Fourteenth Amendment. Ambler's claim was ultimately rejected. The Supreme Court upheld Euclid's police power over land use which affected the village's health, safety, and general welfare.

The Euclid opinion laid down three principles that have shaped all subsequent zoning litigation:

1. The Court emphasized that the scope of police power was valid and should be sufficiently elastic to meet the complex needs of an urbanizing society.
2. Challenges based upon dollar loss in property values would not be sustained on that ground alone and decrease in value would henceforth be considered as only one factor in determining a community interest versus the landowner's interest in property use.
3. The Court extended the validity of community zoning beyond what it had previously been.[6]

As Babcock and Bosselman further indicate, these principles tipped the scales of zoning litigation in favor of local governments and against landowners and, as subsequent developments indicate, against regional interests as well.[7]

The second landmark case was the Nectow case decided by the United States Supreme Court in 1928.[8] In the Nectow case, the landowner agreed that zoning was a proper and valid governmental function for the City of Cambridge (Mass.) to exercise. However, he alleged that the zoning ordinances which applied to his property deprived him of reasonable use of his land and that this represented an uncompensated "taking." The U.S. Supreme Court ruled in favor of the landowner, opining that the Cambridge zoning ordinance failed to promote the health and general welfare of the residents of that area. The Nectow case added to the zoning power principles the rule that unreasonableness of a zoning ordinance, as applied to a specific parcel, was grounds for a constitutional challenge. However, the case indicated that persons seeking to challenge local zoning had to document that they suffered some injury which was more serious than that suffered by residents of the community generally. This ruling meant that only immediate landowners whose property was submitted for rezoning and property owners of abutting parcels had the right to challenge specific zoning ordinances. The burden of proof to document a loss was, of course, on the landowner.

The evaluation and development of local land-use regulations has taken shape over the many decades subsequent to these cases. The referents of local authority responded to many issues which have flowed out of an even more complex urban environment. The factors shaping and limiting local land use have stemmed in large part from the concerns of environmentalists and proponents of open housing. The environmentalists have charged that municipalities cannot provide rational treatment for ecological systems which transcend local boundaries. They also charge that local jurisdictions often have narrow self-interests which are detrimental to the combined interests of urban communities within metropolitan areas. The proponents of open housing have charged that municipal land-use regulations often operate to exclude the residency of low-income persons. Thus, many municipalities deny the poor a reasonable opportunity for residential mobility and subject them to unreasonable burdens through the use of land-use authority. In many areas, low-income persons cannot afford to reside in the communities where they are employed. They are often denied residency because the local land-use regulations prohibit the construction of the types of housing within their economic reach.

There is no set of court cases providing a clear set basis for the reentry of the states into land-use control. Rather, a series of assaults upon local land-use authority from various sources has laid the foundation for the states' recent activity. The legal profession, through its prestigious American Law Institute (ALI) Model Land Development Code, has charged that local land-use decisions need to be "legalized" rather than be composed of ad hoc or piecemeal local decision making.[9] The ALI Code sets forth a detailed model for state machinery via planning, state regulation, and administrative review of local land-use decisions. The federal government has also put pressure upon states to become more involved in land-use policy by instituting the A-95 review process which calls for implementation of land use actions consistent with metropolitan comprehensive plans.[10] The A-95 review is a requirement whereby localities seeking federal grants must submit their grant requests to metropolitan planning agencies for review. If local grant requests are not consistent with metropolitan plans, such metropolitan planning agencies will advise the federal government not to fund the grant applications by way of denying A-95 "clearance." Although the A-95 review is only advisory, it influences the states to guide localities in land-use planning or to have the states create metropolitanwide A-95 review agenices. In addition, states have subsequently created their own A-95 review process as a requirement that must be met if localities are to receive grants from the state. Many state grants to localities for such items as subsidized housing, water and sewers, and highways must be subjected to a state A-95 review process.

The various assaults upon local land-use policy have had the cumulative effect of drawing the states into land-use policy. Just how the states are to be involved has not yet fully unfolded. It is obvious that states cannot and do not want to get involved in the thousands of minor land-use decisions currently decided at local levels. The states need to confront those land-use decisions that are truly major and affect populations of whole urban areas, such as power plant siting, critically sensitive environmental areas, and major capital improvements such as airports and sewers. As Bosselman and Callies indicate, the problem of isolating the types or areas of development that have a significant state or regional impact does not seem amenable to easy solution.[11] The states have started to enjoin the issues of land-use policy, and their approaches not only vary but are at different stages of development.

An additional issue related to land-use planning has surfaced in the last decade: the questions of growth and growth management. Traditionally, Americans have believed the conventional wisdom that growth is good as such, that population and economic growth are undeniably linked, and that as long as there is growth there is the potential for public and private betterment. Although the environmentalists have been in the forefront of attacking the "growth ethic," they have not been alone. Scholars, public officials, and citizens in communities across the country have joined the argument, articulating the idea that nongrowth, or at least managed growth, is becoming more and more attractive. Nongrowth is seen by some as a ploy of the middle-income groups to prevent those less well off from climbing the economic ladder. But in many local communities, growth is increasingly identified with higher taxes, crowded classrooms, congested roads, and overloaded sewer systems. Growth management is practiced at the local level through zoning and planning and such ad hoc measures as sewer moritoria. A number of communities have managed to control population growth outright by limitations on residential building. The City of Petaluma, California was ultimately upheld by the courts in its ordinance which restricted the number of subdivisions of five houses or more that could be built in a year. The town of Ramapo, New York accomplished the same goal by restricting development for which there were not adequate facilities available. Since the approval of both these local procedures in the courts, numerous other small- and medium-sized communities have enacted similar ordinances. Outright attempts to control population growth have been virtually nonexistent at the state level—unless we count Oregon's public relations attempt to scare away permanent in-migration. Billboards, bumper stickers, and newspaper accounts trumpeting the slogan "Don't Californiate Oregon" indicate the state's concern with unbridled growth. Nevertheless, the issue of state land-use control ultimately must contend with the issue implicit in growth, managed growth, and nongrowth.

STATE INVOLVEMENT: NO PANACEA

Control over land use, whether at local, state, or national levels, involves the balancing of a multitude of private and public interests. The reorganization of this complex of public and private land use must occur under more forceful state regulation, even though the interests at work here cannot always be clearly distinguished, neither by the public nor by the experts. The probable results of such state involvement may not be as clear as reformers predict. The Ralph Nader Study Group on land use and the politics of land offers a perspective on why land-use control should be moved from the local to the state level.[12] The report contends that large corporations, wealthy landowners, and developers dominate local land-use decisions, and it recommends that local land-use powers should be curtailed by more state activity and control in land-use matters. However, the results of expanded state land-use controls may not necessarily mean that large corporations, speculators, or developers will be less influential in land-use decisions.

As Frank Popper has argued, the idea that land-use reform can actually be effected by states in this way may well be an illusion, for the same corporate interests that dominate local land-use decisions have long since penetrated state governments as well.[13] According to him, would-be land-use reformers like Ralph Nader, who call for such state control, do not take into account the possibility that forces they wish to control—large corporations, wealthy landowners, greedy developers, polluters, and racists—are likely to be as strong at higher levels of government as at the local level.[14] For example, as of 1971, the development interests had 235 full-time lobbyists in the California State Capitol while conservationists had only 3 lobbyists. More than half the state legislators received income from land dealings in one way or another.[15]

Popper further argues that the proposals of reformers exemplify a general trend in land-use practice—that of expanding the powers, particularly the regulatory powers, of higher levels of government, so as to bypass local bottlenecks and resistance.[16] For the consequence of local control is that development is often not really controlled, but merely displaced by default into neighboring territory that lacks control. Further, the "quality" of land-use control is extremely low in many communities. Zoning and subdivision regulations are often implemented in a haphazard manner. But the trend to greater state regulation over land use does not automatically mean either that all interests will get a fair hearing or that regulations will be evenly applied throughout the state. Land-use regulation is a complex issue to resolve at any level of government. Creating additional and more powerful state agencies may not give community interests the equal access to state decision makers that it does to private developers, since special interests may capture state land-use agencies as easily as they have influenced local governments. State government must therefore be involved in such a way that public and private interests can resolve land-use issues without exclusive control by either interest.

It is to prevent such unilateral control of land use, and thus to resolve matters of negative spillovers among localities by bringing greater rationality to metropolitan development, that reformers have argued for state involvement. And though states have become more actively involved, their objectives do not seem to coincide with the reformers' intentions. It appears, in fact, that state land-use objectives actually coincide much more with the usual local ones—since, as suggested above, the interests that affect local land-use decisions are often identical to those that influence the state. This has been corroborated by a recent study that surveyed the directors of the fifty states' land-use planning agencies as to what they believed were their states' land-use planning objectives.[17] Their views are summarized in Table 6-1. As it shows, protection of individual property rights is the leading objective, with twenty-eight (56%) of the directors giving it primacy. Economic issues followed, with eighteen (36%) of the planners saying these constituted the most important concern. The other three objectives—environmental protection, low-income housing, and growth strategy—were rarely stated as the most important objectives.

Thus it appears that property rights protection and economic growth are political requirements for a successful land-use planning initiative.[18] Moreover, it does not appear that the greater provision and distribution of low-income housing that reformers hoped for will be a prominent objective in state land-use policy. Yet the survey does indicate that state involvement in land-use planning is gaining in importance.[19] What must be kept in mind, however, is that such planning on the state level is going to be subject to political forces similar to those shaping local decisions. These forces will, of course, differ from state to state, depending on their individual demographic, ecological, and economic characteristics.

Table 6.1 Planners' Evaluation of Land-use Legislative Objectives

	Protection of individual property rights	Environment protection	Provision for low-income housing	Growth strategy	Economic issues
Alabama	5	1*	3	2	4
Alaska	4	2	3	1*	5
Arizona	5	2	1	3	4
Arkansas	5	2	1	3*	4*
California	3	5	1	3*	5*
Colorado	5	3	2	1*	4
Connecticut	4	3	2	1*	5
Delaware	1	4*	1	3*	5
Florida	1	4*	2	3*	5
Georgia	1	4	3	2	5
Hawaii	1	3	4	2*	5
Idaho	5	2	2	3	4
Illinois	5	2	1	4*	3
Indiana	5	4	1	2	3
Iowa	5	4	1	2	3
Kansas	5	3	1	2*	4
Kentucky	5	3	1	2*	4
Louisiana	3	2*	1	5	4
Maine	2	4	2	2	4

State Involvement: No Panacea / 127

Maryland	5	2	1	3	4
Massachusetts	1	3	2	4*	5
Michigan	3	2	1	4*	5
Minnesota	5	5	1*	3*	3
Mississippi	4	1*	1*	1*	5
Missouri	5	2	1	4	3
Montana	4	3	2	1	5
Nebraska	5	2	1	3*	4*
Nevada	5	4	1	3	2
New Hampshire	5	1	2	4*	3
New Mexico	5	1	3	2*	4
New York	5	2	1	3	4
North Carolina	4	2	1	3*	5
North Dakota	5	2	1	3*	4*
Ohio	5	3	1	3	4*
Oklahoma	5	3	1	2	4
Oregon	4	3	2	1*	5
Pennsylvania	4*	3	1	2*	5
Rhode Island	2*	3*	1*	5	4
South Carolina	3*	5	2	1	5
South Dakota	5	4	1	3	2
Tennessee	5	3	1	2	4
Texas	5	3	1	3	4
Utah	5	2*	1	4	3
Vermont	5	3*	1	2	4

Table 6.1 (Continued)

	Protection of individual property rights	Environment protection	Provision for low-income housing	Growth strategy	Economic issues
Virginia	5	3	4	3	5
Washington	2	3	1	5	5
West Virginia	1	5	4	2*	3*
Wisconsin	5	3	1	2*	4
Wyoming	1	5	1	5	1
Totals					
Ranked 5 (most important)	28	5	0	4	18
Ranked 4	8	8	3	6	21
Ranked 3	4	19	4	17	8
Ranked 2	3	14	11	15	2
Ranked 1 (least important)	7	4	32	8	1
*(Becoming relatively more important)	2	7	2	19	4

Source: Richard Mann and Mike Miles, "State Land Use Planning," Journal of the American Planning Association 45, no. 1 (1979). Reproduced by permission of the publisher.

STATE LAND-USE APPROACHES

Fred Bosselman and David Callies have described state activity in land-use regulations as the "quiet revolution."[20] This "quiet revolution" began in 1961 in the State of Hawaii. In an attempt to preserve agricultural land to maintain the natural beauty of the islands in the face of urban growth, Hawaii passed a Land Use Law, making the preservation of prime agricultural lands, the guidance of urban growth, and the establishment of a system for prudent management of natural resources its explicit objectives.[21] To achieve these objectives, the law created a State Land Use Commission (LUC) and authorized it to establish the criteria for how land was to be classified throughout the state. On the basis of the resulting classification system, land falls into four use districts: (1) urban districts, which consist of all urban land and reserve land to accommodate urban growth for ten years; (2) rural districts, which include low-density residential developments of half-acre lots; (3) agricultural districts, which include prime agricultural crop lands and grazing land; and (4) conservation districts, which include the basic natural resources. In the urban districts zoning is done by the counties, following LUC regulations; in the other three districts, land use is regulated directly by the LUC.

Thus, in giving the state the power to guide land use in urban localities and to determine it directly everywhere else, Hawaii's Land Use Law has bestowed an unprecedented degree of land-use control upon the state government. This has made Hawaii's land-use program the strongest among all the states.[22]

And though Hawaii still has the most comprehensive program, other states have also made significant moves to direct land-use control. Encouraged by Hawaii's example, several states—California, Oregon, Wisconsin, Florida, Vermont, Maine, and Massachusetts— have passed legislation and created agencies directly controlling various facets of land use. California's Coastal Zone Conservation Commission since 1972 has had a mandate to regulate land use along some 1000 miles of the coastal region. Delaware's Coastal Zone Act, an excellent example of direct state regulation of land use, regulates all industrial development within a one- to six-mile zone along the Delaware Bay Coast and the Atlantic Coast. Oregon requires local consistency with statewide goals and provides for state assumption of planning if there is no local activity. Florida requires local comprehensive planning and, like Michigan and Maryland, regulates areas designated to be of critical state concern. Vermont, through the use of a state board and nine district commissioners, regulates specific types of use throughout the state and requires a state permit for developments in excess of 10 acres. Maine requires a state permit for developments in excess of 20 acres. Although the movement toward increased state involvement is clearly perceptible, the spread of state-level land-use involvement among the fifty states is quite uneven. Several states have not considered, and some states have rejected, state legislation to expand state control of land use. There has not exactly been a nationwide stampede to adopt new legislation for state control over land use.

Two states are involved in land-use control by delegating state regulatory authority not to local governments but to metropolitan regional agencies. The Twin Cities Metropolitan Council of Minneapolis-St. Paul, composed of 7 counties and 321 local government units, is organized as a planning agency rather than a unit of government. The council, created in 1967, reviews and approves development plans of all independent boards, commissions, and agencies in the metropolitan area on the basis of metropolitan development criteria. The Hackensack Meadowlands Development Commission, created in 1968 by the New Jersey Legislature, controls a 20,000-acre district including 14 northern New Jersey municipalities in Bergen and Hudson counties. The commission has the authority to acquire and develop land, adopt a master development plan, conduct special assessments, undertake redevelopment projects, establish comprehensive zoning standards, and issue permits for construction throughout the region. All municipalities in the region share in the financial benefits of development in the area.

As we have argued, land use is a highly political issue, with many interests competing to protect land use. Not insignificant is the fact that land use is considered a cherished local "right" and state control an infringement. The movement of states into this activity has been impeded by several factors. The recession of 1975 and the slowdown of growth in several regions of the country, such as the Northeast and Midwest, have damped aggressive state land regulation. Increased fuel costs, which have led to greater efforts for discovery and development of energy resources such as oil and coal, have affected state efforts. The case of environmentalists for protecting land has been weakened by the increased need for energy development. In addition, slow economic growth or outright decline in growth have placed a damper upon attracting industry and commerce. Rather than regulating growth for the general community "good," which often translates into protecting environmental and aesthetic concerns, several states have been cautious in altering land-use regulations for fear of repelling industry.

While there have been several states (California, Florida, and Oregon) that followed Hawaii in adopting a statewide land-use policy framework at one blow, the majority of states taking action in land-use issues have moved cautiously and in an incremental fashion. This means that most states have not adopted a comprehensive land-use policy. Rather, states have adopted selected land-use policies in areas where political support existed. These are areas where overriding concerns for public safety and resources are involved. For example, as shown in Table 6.2, twenty states have adopted wetlands protection laws; twenty-four states have passed floodplains management legislation; approximately two-thirds of the states have some form of regulation or guidelines for siting power-generation facilities; and an additional thirteen states have land-use programs for designating critical areas that warrant protection for ecological, recreational, or significant resource reasons.[23]

Table 6.2 indicates that all fifty states are involved in some forms of land-use planning. All have local zoning and enabling legislation delegating various degrees of responsibility to local governments and regional agencies. All states have some form of state-level agency, program, or control mechanism dealing with some land-use activity. However, only a few states can boast either a statewide land-use management program or a coordination process that approaches comprehensiveness. Land-use planning is by and large a fragmented assortment of functions carried on at several levels of government with little interagency or intergovernmental coordination.[24]

There is no discernible pattern as to what types of states have the most comprehensive land-use policies. Only five states—Florida, Hawaii, Maine, New York, and Vermont—have a comprehensive statewide permit system. Thus neither the large urban states nor the small rural states have been the leaders. It therefore appears that, in these five states, state action has been stimulated by their own specific state and local political conditions. There is no nationwide trend based upon the pressures of urbanization which "forces" states to adopt land-use policies. Conditions that are endemic to specific states have sparked the "leaders." As noted, Hawaii initiated its state land-use policy soon after it became a state in 1959. Florida rewrote its entire constitution in 1968 and as part of that effort passed extensive land-use policy especially for ecologically sensitive areas such as the wetlands. In Vermont, new growth demands, unhealthy conditions resulting from raw sewage being dumped into streams, and inadequate septic systems prompted comprehensive land-use programs.

A composite picture of the fifty states displays a great deal of unevenness in the development of statewide land-use policy. The data of Table 6.2 illustrate the various steps taken by states, but do not indicate how effective land-use implementation is. The land-use legislation may be on the books, but what is not known is how it actually is

Table 6.2 State Land-use Programs

State	Comprehensive permit system (1)	Coordinated incremental (2)	Mandatory local planning (3)	Coastal zone management (4)	Wetlands management (5)	Power plant siting (6)	Surface mining (7)	Designation of critical areas (8)	Differential assessment laws (9)	Floodplain management (10)	Statewide shorelands act (11)
Alabama						X	A			X	
Alaska		X		X		X			B		
Arizona		X				X			A	X	
Arkansas						X	A, B		A	X	
California		X		X		X	X		C	X	
Colorado						X	X		A	X	
Connecticut		X		X	X	X		X	B	X	
Delaware		X		X	X				A		
Florida	X	X	X	X	X	X		X	A, C		X
Georgia		X		X	X		A, B				
Hawaii	X						X	X	B	X	
Idaho			X			X	X		A		
Illinois				X		X	A, B		B	X	
Indiana		X		X			A, B		A	X	
Iowa							A, B		A	X	
Kansas							A, B				
Kentucky							A, B		B		
Louisiana				X	X	X					
Maine	X	X	X (ltd.)	X	X	X	A	X	B	X	
Maryland		X		X	X	X	A, B	X	B	X	
Massachusetts				X	X	X			B		
Michigan				X			X		C	X	X
Minnesota		X		X	X	X	X	X	B	X	X
Mississippi				X	X					X	
Missouri					X	X	X		A	X	
Montana		X	X			X	A, B	X	B	X	
Nebraska			X			X		X	B	X	X
Nevada		X	X			X		X	B		
New Hampshire				X	X	X			B, C		
New Jersey				X	X	X			B	X	
New Mexico		X				X	A		A		
New York	X	X		X	X	X	X	X	B	X	

State	1	2	3	4	5	6	7	8	9	10	11
North Carolina	X			X					X		B
North Dakota									A		A
Ohio			X						A		B
Oklahoma									X		A
Oregon	X	X		X					A	X	B
Pennsylvania				X					A	X	B
Rhode Island	X			X							B
South Carolina				X					A		B
South Dakota									A		A
Tennessee					X				A, B		
Texas									X		B
Utah		X							A		B
Vermont	X	X							X		C
Virginia				X					A, B		B
Washington	X			X					A		
West Virginia									A, B		X
Wisconsin	X			X				X	X		X
Wyoming	X		X						A		

Key to columns:
1. State has authority to require permits for certain types of development.
2. State-established mechanism to coordinate state land-use-related problems.
3. State requires local governments to establish a mechanism for land use planning (e.g., zoning, comprehensive plan, planning commission).
4. State is participating in the federally funded coastal zone management program authorized by the Coastal Zone Management Act of 1972.
5. State has authority to plan or review local plans or the ability to control land use in the wetlands.
6. State has authority to determine the siting of power plants and related facilities.
7. State has statutory authority to regulate surface mines. (A) State has adopted rules and regulations. (B) State has issued technical guidelines.
8. State has established rules, or is in the process of establishing rules, regulations, and guidelines for the identification and designation of areas of critical concern (e.g., environmentally fragile areas, areas of historical significance.
9. State has adopted tax measure which is designed to give property tax relief to owners of agricultural or open space lands. (A) Preferential assessment program—assessment of eligible land is based upon a selected formula, which is usually use-value. (B) Deferred taxation—assessments of eligible land is based upon a selected formula, which is usually use-value and provides for a sanction, usually the payment of back taxes, if the land is converted to a noneligible use. (C) Restrictive agreements—eligible land is assessed at its use value, a requirement that the owner sign a contract, and a sanction, usually the payment of back taxes if the owner violates the terms of the agreement.
10. State has legislation authorizing the regulation of floodplains.
11. State has legislation authorizing the regulation of shorelands of significant bodies of water.

Source: Based on Council of State Governments, Land Use Planning Report, 1974 and Land Use Planning Report, 1975, and on information collected by the U.S. Department of the Interior, Office of Land Use and Water Planning, and the Resource Land Investigations Program. Data compiled October 1975.

used to shape land-use decisions. It may well be that some states that are considered leaders in land-use policy are not effectively using state authority. What we can say at this point is that all states have demonstrated some initiative, innovation, and accomplishment in some facets of land use, but that no single state, with the exception of Hawaii, has yet produced a truly comprehensive land-use policy.

John DeGrove has offered a typology which classifies states as to the extent of their involvement in land use.[24] DeGrove indicates that there are several approaches that states can follow in land-use policy and that local political conditions determine the directions taken by the various states. He sees land-use policy as the direct result of politics at several distinct stages of the entire process. There is the politics of gestation—the development of those problems and issues that were perceived by groups and individuals to demand strong state action in the land-use area; the politics of adoption—those forces, governmental and private, that opposed on the one hand and supported on the other, the approval of a strong state initiative; the politics of implementation—the major political developments during the period in which new land use initiatives were being carried out; and the politics of the future—an effort to anticipate what will happen with regard to state initiative in the land-use area over the next decade or so.[25] In essence, there may be several routes, all shaped by politics, by which a state may become a "leader" in land-use management.

DeGrove examines land use in the three states of Oregon, California, and Florida, and indicates a range of approaches to policy development. These three states represent positions on a state land-use initiative continuum ranging from a broad general assertion of state authority (Oregon); to a strong assertion of state control in a particular geographic area, the Coast (California); and finally to a strong but selective application of state land use throughout an entire state (Florida).[26] Although analysis has been concentrated on Oregon, California, and Florida, there are many variations on how the remaining forty-seven states approach land use and the successes and failures that are to be found across a wide range of states. All states are moving into "land-use" policy at varying speeds and with differing impacts. It is a development which will become more articulated as it unfolds in the 1980s.

The states vary significantly on how far they have proceeded with a land-use policy. The central issue we have argued in this chapter is that land use is now generally accepted as an issue for state policy. Land use is no longer considered exclusively a local prerogative based upon an "inherent local right." In the past, the states delegated land-use control to localities, and there is no question that they are now reassessing their authority. How states approach land-use "policy" will vary significantly because the states have different objectives, problems, and resources with which to work. Land-use policy will provide an interesting policy framework within which to assess state activity in the metropolitan context.

We see the metropolitan area as the prime factor in state land-use policy during the present decade. The only alternatives for future land use in metropolitan areas are (1) maintaining the status quo, with disjointed land use by competing local governments each "doing its own thing" and (2) encouraging, facilitating, coordinating, and possibly further mandating metropolitan areawide land use by the state (or by the stronger, more visible hand of the federal government). The authors perceive state control of land use as the most attractive of these alternatives, particularly in the metropolitan areas, but all the implications of such a change are as yet unclear. State land-use control very probably is an "idea whose time has come"—but how much will it help? Or will it hurt? There are still too few examples and too few evaluations to be sure.

NOTES

1. Commonwealth of Pennsylvania, Land Policy Strategies Conference Draft, Harrisburg, Pa., September 1977, p. A-6.
2. Nelson Rosenbaum, Land Use and the Legislatures (Washington, D.C.: The Urban Institute, 1976), p. 1.
3. For an examination of local land-use authorities see Randall Scott, ed., Management and Control of Growth (Washington, D.C.: Urban Land Institute, 1975), especially vol. 1, chap. 4, pp. 179-302.
4. Richard Babcock and Fred P. Bosselman, Exclusionary Zoning: Land Use Regulation and Housing in the 1970's (New York: Praeger, 1973), chap. 2.
5. Village of Euclid v. Ambler Realty Co., 272 U.S. 365 (1926).
6. Richard F. Babcock and Fred P. Bosselman, "Land Use Controls: History and Legal Status," in Management and Control of Growth, ed. Randall Scott (Washington, D.C.: Urban Land Institute, 1975), vol. 1:197.
7. Ibid.
8. Nectow v. City of Cambridge, 277 U.S. 183 (1928).
9. The American Law Institute, A Model Land Use Code, Chicago, Tentative Draft 3, 1971.
10. William Brussat, "Realizing the Potentials of A-95," Planning 37, no. 2 (1971).

11. Fred Bosselman and David Callies, The Quiet Revolution in Land Use Control (Washington, D.C.: Council on Environmental Quality, 1971).
12. Ralph Nader Study Group Report on Land Use in California, Politics of Land, Robert C. Fellmath, project director (New York: Grossman, 1973).
13. Frank J. Popper, "Land Use Reform: Illusion or Reality?" Planning 40, no. 8 (1974):14-19.
14. Ibid., p. 15.
15. Ibid., p. 14.
16. Ibid.
17. Richard A. Mann and Mike Miles, "State Land Use Planning: The Current Status and Demographic Rationale," American Planning Association Journal 45, no. 1 (1979):48-60.
18. Ibid., p. 57.
19. Ibid.
20. Fred Bosselman and David Callies, The Quiet Revolution in Land Use Control, Hawaii Revised Statutes Annotated, chap. 205 (Suppl. 1971).
21. Richard N. Tager, Innovations in State Legislation: Land-Use Management (Washington, D.C.: American Institute of Planners May 1974), p. 5.
22. Ibid., p. 7.
23. This section draws heavily on Council of State Governments, State Growth Management, prepared under the direction of the Office of Community Planning and Development, U.S. Department of Housing and Urban Development (Lexington, Ky., May 1976).
24. John M. DeGrove, "The Political Dynamics of Land and Growth Management in the States," paper delivered at the Southern Political Science Meeting, November 4, 1977.
25. Ibid., p. 8. This section relies exclusively upon John DeGrove's classification of land-use politics.
26. Ibid., p. 7.

Chapter 7

STATE DEVELOPMENT OF URBAN-METROPOLITAN STRATEGIES

INTRODUCTION

In recent years reformers and urbanologists have been calling for the states to develop urban and metropolitan strategies. Many observers not only recognize the potential of states to shape urban areas, but they also acknowledge the accomplishments of states during the last decade. What is not clear is whether states have a planned direction or strategy for dealing with urban areas. Do states have a basic strategy for what they want to accomplish in metropolitan areas? No one denies there have been great increases in state aid to localities. However, increases in state aid to urban areas, as has been the case over the last two decades, have not necessarily been aimed at specific urban objectives. States may not clearly distinguish between urban and nonurban areas as policy is developed. Also, state aid may be narrowly focused and flow along functional lines such as education, highways, and welfare. State assistance for highway construction may facilitate suburban growth, while central-city revitalization funds may be aimed at rebuilding central business districts.

We think it is critical to raise the question of how states attempt to approach the needs of urban areas in a strategic fashion. That is, we ask how much progress have states made in sorting out their urban priorities and whether they have something resembling a policy for urban areas. Moving toward or developing specific policy is an important step for states to take if they are to deal effectively with the multiple causes and consequences of metropolitanization. This perspective takes as given the fact that states have accomplished a great deal in the separate functional areas, and that states have given relatively large amounts of aid to their local units. What we want to focus upon here is how and to what extent states attempt to tie together all the various activities they pursue into an urban policy framework.

We will focus on three distinct comprehensive approaches that states have utilized for dealing with urban and metropolitan areas. The three approaches are the establishment of state departments of community affairs and of state commissions on local governments and the development of urban strategies. The three approaches all have the common characteristic of dealing with urban areas in a generalized and comprehensive fashion and do not take the functional perspective of dealing exclusively with single-issue concerns. The three approaches differ in how they are organized and structured to deal with urban areas. State departments of community affairs are part of the official organization of state governments. The state commissions on local governments are both permanent and temporary study groups which include nongovernmental individuals as well as public officials. The urban strategy approach combines planning and action stimulated by certain states and picked up by the federal government as part of the national urban policy. Although urban strategies originate in the states, it is hoped that their objectives are in concert with federal urban objectives.

STATE DEPARTMENTS OF COMMUNITY AFFAIRS

A relatively new phenomenon in state-local relations is the state-level department of community affairs (DCA). Most states now have some variant of this entity for the purpose of coordinating numerous services to localities or supervising programs on their behalf. We can trace their beginnings to 1956 when the Council of State Governments recommended that each state establish an agency to examine the needs of metropolitan areas and drew up model legislation toward that end. The concept was endorsed by the National Governors Conference, the National League of Cities, the United States Conference of Mayors, and the Advisory Commission on Intergovernmental Relations (ACIR). The creation of such groups gained real momentum in 1966 when Congress passed the Demonstration Cities Act which authorized grants for the establishment of such agencies. Although there is some argument over which state established the first such agency, New York has claimed credit for its State Office of Local Government, created in 1959. By 1967 there were sixteen state agencies for local affairs, and as of 1978 there were forty-five agencies; only five states (Hawaii, Maine, Nevada, New Hampshire, and North Dakota) do not have a DCA-type agency with broad responsibilities in local assistance.[1]

The New York State Office of Local Government surveyed the other agencies regarding their activities as of 1973, and the results were reported in the 1975 report of the Pennsylvania-sponsored conference on "The States' Role in Strengthening Local Government

Capabilities."[2] According to the survey, the activities of such agencies fall into four major types. The first and most common activity is technical assistance and advisory services, which includes assistance in finance, laws and legislation, management and organization, interlocal cooperation, coordination of state activities affecting local governments, and research and data collection.

A second area is that of planning services, including functional planning, regional planning coordination, and planning assistance in such areas as zoning, land use, and official maps. Results of the survey indicate that thirty-four states have assigned some form of program responsibility in this area to the state agency for local affairs. Supervision of local finances, state and federal aid, and personnel training make up a third area of activities for the state agencies. Of the forty-two agencies responding, forty reported offering assistance on state and federal aid programs, twenty-nine reported municipal training activities, and seven have a supervisory-type responsibility for local finances.

The final area of activity is community and human resource development, which includes involvement in federal and state housing, urban renewal, antipoverty, and economic development programs. Of the forty-two state agenices, eleven reported a responsibility for urban renewal; twenty were involved in model cities programs; nineteen had antipoverty programs; thirty-two had some housing activities; and twenty-nine reported an economic development responsibility.

State departments of community affairs are undertaking many types of functions, from offering advice to assuming some type of control or supervision over programs. The newest efforts have been performance monitoring, supervision of state-local programs, and action as a liaison between the state and local governments.[3] The origins of these departments lie in a state's traditional role— provision of technical assistance to local governments—but many of these agencies have lacked financial and statutory support and do not take a comprehensive approach to urban areas.[4]

Despite these shortcomings there is growing consensus that all states should have some type of agency for local affairs. Grant calls them an encouraging mechanism for reducing federal-state tensions.[5] However, most state-local government administrative supervision takes place along functional lines, with the activities of particular local governments being the objects of concern of state agencies with similar substantive responsibilities. The level of professionalism, the amount of resources, and the extent of authority among departments of community affairs vary significantly among the states. The DCAs perform many functions for local government, most commonly in the area of improving general local government planning and improvement.

Among the DCA functions, several have the impact of integrating diverse state activities into more coherent urban policy. The DCAs perform research and policy analysis on the states' urban problems and local governmental performance. The DCAs also act as an information clearinghouse for local governments and coordinate certain state services and assistance programs. DCAs often serve as the liaison between federal and state agencies and local governments, both as mobilizers of federal-state resources and as local government advocates for needed federal and state policy changes.

The record of accomplishment of DCAs as an urban policy-integrating mechanism is spotty. DCAs are developing organizations of state government that provide a formal state context for pursuing multifaceted urban policies. Although DCAs currently emphasize assistance to the smaller communities, they are broadening their role to assist the larger jurisdictions and function as policy brokers for state agencies on urban affairs issues. The Pennsylvania DCA is considered a leader in its efforts to develop an urban policy. It performs research, translates executive guidelines into departmental policies, and evaluates the progress and impacts of state and federal programs. Most DCAs of other states are not as developed as Pennsylvania's in pursuing urban policy. Yet most DCAs are moving in this direction and their progress deserves close attention. As the state-federal partnership evolves, DCAs are likely candidates for the mechanism through which local governments and citizens can influence decision making at the state level as they relate to the formulation of urban policy.

STATE COMMISSIONS ON LOCAL GOVERNMENT

Fifteen state commissions on local government (SCLGs) were created in fourteen states between 1959 and 1973 to examine and make recommendations on urban policy, especially concerning the issues of local governmental organization, service delivery, and state-local relationships (see Table 7.1).[6] The creation of SCLGs was prompted by the severity of urban problems in several states and the recognition that new approaches which included local officials and private citizen input were needed. In contrast to DCAs, which are official organizations of the state, the SCLGs attempt to approach urban policy from a perspective which combines state, local, and nongovernmental concerns.

Although the SCLGs vary in name, structure, membership, composition, duration, and impact on policies, they have a number of characteristics in common.[7] All commissions were established under mandate from either the governor, the legislature, or both. All

Table 7.1 State Commissions on Local Government

State (name of commission)	Creator/scope of commission	Duration	Funding and sources	Membership (a) number (b) appointer (c) member characteristics	Staff characteristics	Accomplishments
California Local Government Reform Task Force	Created by gov.'s executive order/ study reforms for & simplification of over-lapping levels of gov.	1-1/2 yr Nov. 1972- July 1974	Total: $279,000 State: 50,000 State in-kind 32,000 IPA: 35,000 State OEO: 24,000 HUD: 138,000	(a) 7 (b) Governor (c) 5 Republicans 2 Democrats Governor's cabinet acted as steering committee	15 Professionals at peak of work; volunteers used from universities	Reported ideas to governor's cabinet; no bill drafting; no formal studies made
Florida Commission on Local Government	Created by legislative act/examine operation & organization of local gov.	2 yr July 1972- June 1974	$250,000—All state-appropriated	(a) 15 (b) 9 by Governor 3 by House Speaker 3 by President of Senate	Professional staff & executive director; work partly contracted to university personnel	Wrote own legislation; legislator members lobbied; almost 100% passage of bills that were recommended
Illinois Municipal Problems Commission	Created by legislative act/provide liaison between other dept. of state, the legislature, & local municipalities	Permanent 1959-	$60,000/yr Appropriation	(a) 18 (b) Legislature (c) 5 from Senate; 5 from House; 4 from members at large. In legislature, majority party appoints 3 of the 5 members from each house & 2 mayors and 2 members at large; minority party appoints the remainder	1 Executive secretary; staff work contracted	Functions continually as local government's link with the legislature & with state government
Maryland Commission on Functions of Government	Created by legislative act/undertake a comprehensive study of all functions of gov. & identify them as state, local, or joint	3 yr Aug. 1972- July 1975	$150,000—All state-appropriated	(a) 27 (b) Governor (c) Elected county and municipal officials, state admin's, 3 delegates, 3 senators, plus business & civic leaders	Executive director & asst. director full time; 4 other professionals full & part time; 2 clerical; & college interns	1500-Page report; no measurable impact

Table 7.1 (Continued)

State (name of commission)	Creator/scope of commission	Duration	Funding and sources	Membership (a) number (b) appointer (c) member characteristics	Staff characteristics	Accomplishments
Michigan Special Commission on Urban Problems	Created by gov.'s executive order/ study all problems relating to urban areas	7 months 1966-67	$0 All services provided voluntarily by members; printing donated by chairman	(a) 45 members (b) Governor (c) Strictly blue-ribbon, representing all interest groups, local officials, civic groups	Staff director provided by Wayne State University; 3 academic senior advisors; 46 tech. advisors	No measurable impact; governor not up for reelection.
Michigan Special Commission on Local Government	Created by gov.'s executive order/ research and recomm. on state & local fiscal policy and functions of local gov., regionalization; future development policy; & relationship of state & local gov.	17 months Oct. 1970-March 1972	Part: HUD grant	(a) 38 members (b) Governor (c) Municipal officials and administrators, county officials, state administrators, 2 legislators academics, & representatives of associations	4 Executive office staff, 4 consultants	—
Montana Commission on Local Government	Created by legislative act/new constitution required review of Code of Local Government	3-1/2 yr Jan. 1974-July 1977	Total: $300,000 State App.: 250,000 HUD: 40,000 HEW: 10,000	(a) 9 (b) Governor (c) 4 Legislators; 5 Lay persons	22 Professionals including lawyers & political scientists	Has recommended and drafted bills for legislature
New Jersey County Municipal Government Study Commission	Created by legislative act/examine current problems of local gov. & recomm. changes	Permanent 1969-	Total: $130,000 for 1974-$100,000 basic state appropriation annually; $30,030 from state Dept. of Community Devel. for study	(a) 15 (b) 6 from Legislature 3 appointed by head of each house; 9 appointed by governor to include 3 county officials, 3 municipal offices & 3 at-large	4 Professionals, 2 concerned with housing & land use; 2 concerned with environment	Major impact

Commission	Description	Duration	Funding	Membership	Staff	Results
New York Commission on Local Government (Wagner Commission)	Created by gov.'s executive order/ look at structure & function of counties & cities & the distribution of functions	3 yr 1970-1973	Total: $1.6 million (spent $1.2 million returned $400,000)—all allocated from the governor's budget	(a) 18 (b) Governor (c) 9 from Upstate; 9 from downstate; 9 were Republican, 9 Democrats; also represented mayors, county executives, assemblymen & racial/ethnic groups	7 Members, 3 full-time professionals; most work done through consultants	Studies published; Legislation drafted—small percentage passed
New York Commission on New York City (Scott Commission)	Created by legislative act/look at the structure & function of N.Y. City to determine if improvements might be made	2 yr 1971-1973	Approx. $1.1 million all approp. by the legislature; in addition, departments asked for and paid for other, related studies	(a) 5 (b) Governor (c) All nonpolitical prominent citizens of N.Y. City; used task force of other prominent experts & had them report back	15 Members, full-time professionals; used consultants extensively	Studies published; no legislation; New York City Charter Commission followed; made specific recommendations on change in City Charter
North Carolina Local Government Study Commission	Created by joint legislative act/study government structure, powers, public policies, & limitations of local gov. units & make recomm. necessary to maintenance of effective & responsible local gov.	6 yr July 1967 to report in 1969, continued to 1973	$50,000, Governor's Contingency and Emergency Fund	(a) 15 (b) 3 Appointed by Senate president; 6 by House Speaker; and 6 by governor (c) 4 Senators, 6 representatives; 3 local government officials, 1 academician, & 1 businessman	Univ. Inst. of	1 Official study published; drafted bills that were enacted
Ohio Commission on Local Government Services	Created by gov.'s executive order/ examine allocation of functions among levels of gov.; local gov. financial status & regional gov.	2 yr April 1972-1974	Total $500,000—$100,000 from state appropriations, $375,000 from foundations (Ford, Batelle, Weatherhead, Cleveland, & George Gund); $25,000 state in-kind	(a) 50 (b) Governor (c) Blue-ribbon, balanced regionally, & by major interest groups	Director appointed by governor; 5 professionals, 3 administrative assistants (professionals appointed by staff director)	Little except for reports published; governor not reelected

Table 7.1 (Continued)

State (name of commission)	Creator/scope of commission	Duration	Funding and sources	Membership (a) number (b) appointer (c) member characteristics	Staff characteristics	Accomplishments
South Dakota Local Government Study Commission	Created by legislative act/study the structure of gov. below the state level to determine ways & means for a more efficient & economic local gov.	Permanent April 1968–	Annual state approp.; act authorized $10,000; various approp. from $13,500 to $18,000	(a) 15 (b) Governor and legislative leadership (c) 4 Local gov. officials & 1 academician by governor; 6 representatives & 4 senators	Legislative research council staffs	Drafts specific legislation, most of which has been enacted
Texas Urban Development Commission	Created by gov.'s executive order/ study urban problems	1-1/2 yr May 1970– Nov. 1971	$100,000 Government office in-kind; Texas foundations	(a) 22 (b) Governor (c) Regional & interest-group balance, including legislators, local officials, interest & civic groups	Professional executive director; staffs from Inst. of Urban Studies at U. of Texas at Arlington & same at University of Houston	Published reports; drafted and recommended about 25 pieces of legislation—90% passed; state ACIR created
Virginia Metropolitan Areas Study Commission	Created by gov.'s executive order/ study laws on annexation & problems of all metropolitan areas and offer solutions	1-1/2 yr 1966–1967	$100,000 State-appropriated	(a) 12 (b) Governor (c) Regional balance; legislators, former legislators, business & universities	Professional staff director; 1 subcommittee staff from Inst. of Government, Univ. of Virginia, & 1 subcommittee staff from D.C. consulting firm	Wrote studies; made legislative proposals of which all were passed due to the strength of the governor
Wisconsin Citizens Commission on Metropolitan Problems	Created by gov.'s executive order/ study restraints on local gov. & concepts which decrease their effectiveness	21 months May 1971– Jan. 1973	$124,000 Wisconsin Dept. of Community Development Budget	(a) 15 (b) Governor (c) Balanced interest groups	3 Full-time professionals assisted by Dept. of Community Development	Nothing substantial; in fact, some say a "futile" effort

Source: Compiled by authors on the basis of telephone interviews and Commission reports and publications.

commissions possess a measure of independence from those who established them; all have some members who are not government policymakers; and all issue a final report which presumably serves as a basis for policy debate and formulation.

These commissions are generally separate from other state institutions, the exception being those that function as adjuncts to the legislature and report directly to it. Commission membership includes a mix of unpaid citizens, public officials, and state legislators. Funding comes from private sector contributions, grants from foundations or the federal government, a single state appropriation, an annual state appropriation, or a combination of these.

Before the SCLGs, the most common approach for developing state urban policy had been along functional service lines, such as education or transportation, with local government activities being the primary concern of state agencies with similar substantive responsibilities. The SCLGs differ from other approaches in that they attempt to establish policy on local and metropolitan reorganization and service delivery comprehensively throughout the state. The commission approach takes into account that contemporary state policy, formed over decades, may have accumulated inconsistent and sometimes contradictory solutions to state-local issues.

Academic literature indicates that governmental commissions are created for numerous reasons, some of which have nothing to do with offering feasible policy alternatives.[8] The role and eventual impact of commissions has been assessed as lying in one of two directions: (1) in the early stages of the policy process, they provide input such as new ideas, articulation of the interests of various groups, public expression of possible courses of action, and model bills for the legislature to consider; or (2) they are used as mechanisms to defuse, defer, or stop actions on complicated conflict issues. Governmental commissions have been accused of studying a problem in the hope that the problem will cool down during the course of the study. The recommendations of such commissions are not adopted into public policy.

Commission Recommendations

There is surprising similarity in the recommendations of SCLGs. They offer, in language ranging from the general to the very specific, what we call the "litany" of reform, a shopping list of "good government" and reorganization changes that can be traced to the reports issued during the last fifteen years by the Advisory Commission on Intergovernmental Relations (ACIR) or the various studies done by the Committee on Economic Development over roughly the same period.[9] The "litnay" is grounded in the assumptions that there is duplication, overlap, and waste in local government; that there is a need for areawide governmental cooperation and/or organizations and areawide delivery of certain services; and that the state must assume a more positive role in guiding local government reorganization and setting service delivery standards, while at the same time encouraging and enhancing home rule in a maximum number of local governmental activities.

Specifically, the shopping list includes state enabling legislation for many of the alternatives we discussed in Chap. 4, such as allowing local governments to consolidate; encouraging or discouraging the creation of special districts; strengthening regional or areawide delivery of services; modernizing county government; establishing state boundary review commissions; and improving fiscal administration and conditions of tax equity.

Both structural and operational fiscal recommendations were present in every report. They took several forms, of which the primary was tax equity. States were enjoined to revise revenue-sharing formulas, to give localities more flexible taxing and borrowing authority, to vary local revenue structures, to change local debt limits, and to institute a version of the circuit breaker in property tax administration. Improved financial management was the other major aspect of fiscal concerns. Recommended were uniform state financial reporting requirements and purchasing procedures for the localities.

The creation of new agencies or executive departments figured prominently in the recommendations. State boundary commissions, departments of local government services or community affairs, and planning agencies or departments were proposed in over half of the reports. Additionally, commissions recommended structural changes in regional substate districts and sought multicounty planning districts where none existed.

The most common recommendation regarding local government structure was to strengthen or modernize county governments. States were urged to grant home rule to counties, to establish county executives or county manager positions, to grant legislative power to counties—all measures designed to grant counties additional authority. Counties were considered either as more in need of "modernization" than cities or as the top tier of a two-tier metropolitan area local government system. Thus it was suggested that both counties and municipalities be granted the authority, through local referenda, to modify their forms of government, the terms of officeholders, the salaries of officials, and election regulations.

Encouraging interlocal cooperation was a general theme of the recommendations. The states were urged to play a more positive role in assisting local government through assumption of some portion of the increased fiscal burdens of local government. Commissions also recommended higher standards for areawide service delivery and more direct state involvement in local boundary change decisions.

Adoption of Recommendations

Legislative adoption of commission recommendations can be used as a standard for assessing their immediate impact, even though commissions may have impact in the long run even if their recommendations are not enacted into law immediately. It may, for example, well be the case that a commission's recommendations are more farsighted than the legislature's perception of immediate needs or that legislators might feel that acting upon some recommendations might prove impolitic or unpopular at the moment. It is therefore difficult, if not impossible, to demonstrate a commission's impact years after it has ceased to function. Many factors will have intervened between the publication of a commission's recommendations and the adoption at a later time of similar laws by the legislature.

The nature and severity of the urban problem leading to the creation of the commission will thus affect the adoption of recommendations. In states which created commissions to respond to generalized urban problems, the SCLG recommendations were also general. The SCLGs in California, Michigan, Ohio, Wisconsin, and New York were all created to study broadly the reform of local government. Their recommendations were rarely adopted by legislatures. In contrast, the Florida and Virginia SCLGs, for example, were created to deal with specific urban and governmental questions. After the creation of these commissions, their mandates were expanded to review local government and metropolitan organization generally, but the resolution of the specific problem remained as a focus amid the general study and recommendations. Thus the nature of the problem shaped the commissions' work. General problems begot general solutions, and specific problems, while assessed within a general framework of local governmental processes, begot specific recommendations.

A commission's relationship with the state legislature also affected the adoption of recommendations. Commissions closely tied to the legislative process, such as those with adjunct status, had the highest rates of adoption of recommendations. Where commissions were created to assist the legislatures with local government organization and service delivery issues, their approach to local government issues was specifically geared to changing state law. They accomplished this in a continuous and incremental fashion over several years. The tradeoff for high adoption of recommendations was that such commissions were more limited in range in their recommendations than the non-adjunct SCLGs. The adjunct commissions approached local governmental issues one problem at a time over several legislative sessions, continuously receiving from the legislature additional problems to study and new requests for recommendations.

Commissions which submitted recommendations in draft bill form had the most immediate impact within the legislature. Recommendations in draft bill form permitted direct input and reaction from the legislature, often in the form of informal feedback prior to submission of final recommendations. Bills, even those that were defeated in the legislature, gave commission recommendations a direct opportunity to be considered, either in committee or on the floor, and were often voted upon by the entire body.

Observations

SCLGs alter the scope of the policy process on local government and metropolitan area reorganization and intergovernmental relations. These commissions permit previously uninvolved interests to enter this process. Representatives of industry, labor, the academic community, and the professions gain access to policymaking, along with the governmental officials. Also, by being on such commissions, local governmental officials can tackle a broad range of state-local relations issues instead of having to deal with one issue at a time, as when testifying on specific legislative matters. In addition, these commissions have the opportunity to review numerous local government functions across a wide spectrum of governmental structures and intergovernmental relationships. Whether the state commissions are designed for specific policy purposes or to act as a more general study group, they are a metropolitan area's state-local policy mechanism functioning within the larger state political environment. Because partisan interests and conflict between the executive branch and legislature condition SCLG creation and their eventual impact, SCLGs are also responsive to many of the broader issues and pressures which emanate from and affect the governor and legislatures.

There is a consensus as to what local government and intergovernmental reform shall be pursued. The "litany of reform" is fairly consistent across the states we have examined, the only exception being California. The reason for such similarity appears to lie in the fact that the SCLG does not do original work. It takes its perspectives and framework for analysis from others, including other SCLGs, but most notably from the Advisory Commission on Intergovernmental Relations and the Committee for Economic Development, which are the synthesizers of much of traditional reform scholarship.[10]

There is a great deal of variation, however, among the states in the severity of the urban problems that they confront and the political environments within which intergovernmental relations are shaped. Cooperation and conflict among governments exists not only between levels of governments, such as state-local, but among governments at the same level, such as among localities in metropolitan areas and among the governor, state agencies, and the legislature and SCLGs at the state level.

Astute political participants can utilize the SCLG to help solve complex urban problems. Commissions such as those in Florida and Montana have altered urban and metropolitan area intergovernmental relations considerably. SCLGs which view urban areas in broad general terms as "in need of reform" do not produce recommendations which are adopted. As general reform is translated into specific recommendations, the likelihood of its implementation increases.

FEDERAL AND STATE URBAN STRATEGY

With the articulation of the president's "Urban Policy" in 1978, the executive branch of the federal government also added its voice to the call for more state visibility in urban and metropolitan areas. One of the nine major proposals which comprised the president's urban program was the State Community Conservation and Development-State Urban Strategies Incentive Grants. The bill would have authorized grants to states as incentives to develop comprehensive strategies and state-initiated governmental reforms to provide assistance to communities experiencing distress or decline.

Although the Incentive bill was not enacted by Congress, the Department of Housing and Urban Development (HUD), using the Comprehensive Planning Assistance (701) Program, initiated a system of incentive funding which made grants to states and regional planning organizations that had taken the lead in actually developing and implementing strategies to assist cities and distress places. HUD received applications from twenty-four states of which nine were funded and from seventy regional planning organizations of which ten were funded.[11]

The federal approach, as funded by HUD 701 Planning monies, is an example of state action which results from a federal push. New here is the federal attempt to come to grips with states and their local governments through a federal agenda. The federal government is putting pressure on states to develop urban strategies concerned primarily with distressed areas and their localities. For when the states have dealt with problems of localities or urban and metropolitan areas, they have generally made policy either comprehensively for all jurisdictions or selectively in certain functional areas such as education, and have not usually singled out the distressed or disadvantaged as targets of their efforts. The federal government's objective is thus to push states to develop strategies specifying additional assistance for such disadvantaged people in such areas. Such a policy may find some success in the Northeast and some midwestern states which have distressed areas such as Newark, New Jersey, Buffalo, New York, or Detroit, Michigan. But many other states, particularly in the West and South, are less responsive in that their urban centers are not severely distressed. And as long as the federal government commits only small resources, as in the case of this program, the state will adopt such federal urban policies only to the extent that they coincide with their own goals. These goals vary according to the state under consideration.

Initially, the concept of a national urban policy may have been picked up as an idea from some of the states themselves. As with so many national policies, State Urban Strategies was originally an idea that sprang from the policy activities of an innovative state. In this case, three states are credited with developing the urban strategy approach and getting the federal government to adopt it as a national urban policy, namely, California, Massachusetts, and Michigan. Journalist Neal R. Pierce remarked in 1978, "If I were to select an event which has (1) captured attention in Washington and (2) shown the inherent capacity to act of state government, I would select the emergence into national view in the past year of the state urban policies of Massachusetts, Michigan, California and a handful of other states."[12]

Basically what California, Massachusetts, and Michigan accomplished was to design a comprehensive strategy for their urban areas in consultation with state, local, and private interests. In each state, the governor became committed to the concept and applied substantial political power to effect a definable state urban strategy. The urban strategies of the three states had different themes which reflected their respective major concerns. In California the dominant theme of the strategy was to contain urban sprawl. In Massachusetts it was to reinforce and assist existing town and city centers. In Michigan the primary concern was to make increased fiscal resources available to depressed areas and neighborhoods.

Although the themes differed among the three states, their development of an urban strategy did indicate not only that states could take the initiative but that they could define the problems that were most pressing to them and chart a course for their solution. It is still too early to determine whether these urban strategies will be backed by the necessary resources to make them effective in dealing with urban problems. It must be recognized that the fruits of state urban strategies could be long in ripening fully: political, legal, and financial constraints often present formidable obstacles to the implementation of even the best-designed urban strategies.

The recent state development of urban strategies illustrates that the federal government cannot force the states into adopting a national strategy designed in Washington. The federal government could and did encourage the states to adopt a strategic approach to their urban areas. However, the states have demonstrated that they will determine whether they will adopt a strategy and what objectives they will include in the strategy. The pace of strategy development and the amount of resources to be committed to urban strategies are also determined by the states. The federal government can encourage and assist the states, but it cannot force the states to adopt a national urban strategy.

The recent experience of federal and state governments pursuing urban strategies indicates that it has to be approached as a partnership. Neal Pierce has called the particularities of such a partnership a negotiated federalism.[13] A negotiated federalism implies the initiation of a dialogue between federal and state governments over what states have done and a discussion of shortcomings and possible future actions. This approach is thus not as open-ended as revenue sharing nor as restrictive as categorical aid. In negotiated federalism, the national government does not prescribe state urban policy. Rather, each state would be invited to describe its own existing policies—fiscal, regulatory, and in investment terms—that have either positive or negative effects on urban areas in the state. The state would be asked to name the actions it would agree to take in assisting urban areas. Finally, the states would be invited to identify the criteria by which they want to be evaluated in order to receive federal incentive funding.

CONCLUSIONS

The states have taken several approaches toward comprehensive urban strategies. As states differ, so do their approaches to urban and metropolitan area problems. There is wide variation among the states as to how much progress has been achieved. Different states do not confront the same urban and metropolitan problems. It is not reasonable to expect them to give the same priorities to these areas. The most severe problems of many states do not lie in the metropolis. Rather, many states are most concerned with the economic development of the entire state or assisting local governments.

States are themselves too politically powerful for the federal government to force rigid urban strategies upon them, and states have made a great deal of progress in assisting local areas without federal pressure. The states have become increasingly attentive to urban concerns—particularly over the last decade. Admittedly, state efforts to develop urban strategies are still in the formative stages. While it is still too early to determine whether states' urban strategies will take root and flourish, the approaches described in this chapter represent an encouraging departure from the traditionally lackluster performance of state government in urban areas. To date, the states' accomplishments in strategy development reflect their diversity and their individual resources and needs, as well as the influence of the federal government.[14]

NOTES

1. Joseph S. Marinich and Frank A. Kirk, "Community Affairs," in Book of the States (Lexington, Ky.: Council of State Governments, 1978), pp. 592-99.
2. Commonwealth of Pennsylvania, Department of Community Affairs, "The States' Role in Strengthening Local Government Capacities," report of national conference, September 22-24, 1974.
3. Advisory Commission on Intergovernmental Relations, Improving Urban America: A Challenge to Federalism (Washington, D.C.: U.S. Government Printing Office), pp. 158-89.
4. Frank Kolesar, "The States and Urban Planning and Development," in The States and the Urban Crisis, ed. Alan K. Campbell (Englewood, Cliffs, N.J.: Prentice-Hall, 1970), pp. 115-20.
5. Daniel R. Grant, "The Decline of the States' Rights and the Rise of State Administrations," in The States and the Metropolis. Lee S. Greene, Malcolm E. Jewell, and Daniel R. Grant, eds. (University: University of Alabama Press, 1968), p. 113.
6. Different aspects of this research can be found in Vincent L. Marando and Patricia S. Florestano in State and Local Government Review 9, no. 2 (1977):29-53, and Patricia S. Florestano and Vincent L. Marando in National Civic Review 67, no. 8 (1978): 358-61.
7. Two primary sources of data were used in our analysis of SCLGs: Commission documents and reports from the fifteen commissions constitute the basis for determining selected policy approaches. We have obtained the final or most recent report of each commission. These available reports contain the SCLG analysis of problems, information authorizing the establishment of each commis-

sion, and detailed research issued by each of them. Forty in-depth telephone interviews were conducted with commissioners, staff, and knowledgeable observers of each of the fifteen. At least one and as many as four interviews were obtained concerning each commission. The interviews dealt with reasons for the establishment of the commissions, the type of interests represented by commissioners, and the impact of the commission recommendations, as well as the general process of using commissions on policy mechanisms.

8. For a discussion, see Daniel Bell, "Government by Commissions," Public Interest 3 (Spring 1966):3-9; Martha Derthick, "On Commissionship Presidential Variety," Public Policy 19 (Fall 1974): 623-38; Elizabeth Drew, "On Giving Oneself a Hotfoot: Government by Commission," Atlantic Monthly 221 (May 1968):45-49; Frank Popper, The President's Commissions (New York: Twentieth Century Fund, 1970); and George T. Sulzer, "The Policy Processes and the Use of National Governmental Study Commission," Western Political Quarterly 24 (September 1971): 438-48, esp. 439.

9. Committee for Economic Development, Reshaping Government in Metropolitan Areas (New York, 1970); idem, Modernizing Local Government (New York, 1966); Advisory Commission on Intergovernmental Relations, Urban America and the Federal System (Washington, D.C.: U.S. Government Printing Office, October 1969); idem, Substate Regionalism and the Federal System Series, vol. 1-6 (Washington, D.C.: U.S. Government Printing Office, 1973-74).

10. Ibid.

11. U.S. Department of Urban Development, HUD News, no. 78-379, November 24, 1978.

12. Neal R. Pierce, "A Public Interest Challenge for State Investment Planning," State Planning Issues 2, no. 2 (1978):8-14.

13. Ibid.

14. Advisory Commission on Intergovernmental Relations, State Community Assistance Initiatives: Innovations of the Late 70's (Washington, D.C.: U.S. Government Printing Office, May 1979).

Chapter 8

THE STATES AND THE METROPOLITAN AREAS: RESEARCH, ISSUES, AND THE FUTURE

INTRODUCTION

The states have not charted clear and purposeful policies for their metropolitan areas. Yet states evidence much less rural bias toward their metropolitan areas than a decade-and-a-half ago. At that time Alan K. Campbell indicated that the states were at the crossroads between continuing to obstruct solutions to urban problems and making great contributions to the solution of urban crisis.[1] States are still at the crossroads. Although their performance has not approached their potential for dealing with metropolitan areas, the direction of their relationships with the metropolis seems clear.

State governments are no longer sick, as charged in the mid-1960s.[2] State legislatures do not continue to overrepresent a political tradition devised for small-town living in the last century. The reapportionment revolution within the states has placed political power in the metropolitan areas; however, it has been the suburban areas which have gained most from reapportionment, not the central cities. Although urban interests are represented in state legislatures, they have not been formulated into metropolitanwide perspectives.

Metropolitan areas have not become creatures of the state. Neither have metropolitan areas become creatures of the federal government, as many in the 1960s thought would happen. The states have kept pace with the federal and local governments in responding to urban and metropolitan needs. Although the empirical evidence for the state impact on urban areas is lacking, there has been a definite shift in mood. The mood has shifted from one of despondency and discontent to one of guarded optimism concerning the role of states in the metropolis. States are no longer whipping boys.

We return to where we began this volume. The actions and impact of state governments on metropolitan areas are not yet adequately understood or known. The states have engaged in a great variety of activities during the past decade; there are numerous catalogs indicating how much progress states have made recently in assisting their communities. But the impact of such activities has not yet been assessed; there is virtually no systematic research which examines the impact of state actions on metropolitan areas. At present there is no internally coherent theory which guides research to assess the role of state governments. States have been referred to as the "strategic middle" or the "keystones" of the American governmental arch. What is known about the impact of state activities has been confined to individual, ad hoc examples of "best" or "worst" state efforts. This perspective is no longer sufficient. Scholars must now reexamine how well, in fact, the states are performing. We need to assess, among other things, the conditions and circumstances which allow the transfer of ideas and policies from one state to another.

Fifty states means fifty state roles. These roles will be shaped by factors which are internal to the fifty states as well as by continued federal influences. The states differ as to size, extent of urban populations, available resources, and severity of problems. States such as New York, New Jersey, and Michigan contain distressed central cities, whereas Oregon's concerns appear primarily to be how to avoid duplicating the mistakes of California, which has experienced rapid growth and urban sprawl. If research on states is to advance beyond the recitation of "good" and "bad" examples of state actions, data must be gathered across the fifty states in accordance with a theoretical perspective which explains what states have achieved and can hope to achieve. Although in-depth research is needed on all fifty states, it should be performed with the guidance of overarching theories that cut across all states and can be used to compare and contrast state activites in urban areas. A research framework should cover the key issues fundamental to an understanding of how states interact with urban communities and the consequences of that interaction. We would like now to discuss some of the issues involved in examining the role of states.

RESEARCH THEMES

Balanced growth and targeting are two primary themes for research into state metropolitan activities. A policy for balanced growth implies that states aid their local communities through broad-gauged coalitions of state-local activities. Balanced growth is a goal that has gained support in virtually every region of the country, in jurisdictions as diverse as Oklahoma, Arizona, Illinois, and Idaho.[3] On preliminary analysis, the balanced-growth approach appears to be pursued to some extent by all states. States which do not have severe urban problems adopt balanced-growth strategies to cover the needs of urban and rural areas alike. The Advisory Commission on Intergovernmental Relations (ACIR) indicates that the widespread use of balanced-growth strategy derives largely from its consensual appeal; the term suggests an inclusive state approach to localities, a willingness to set aside interlocal divisions and to address the needs of all communities within a state, urban and rural alike.

Targeting is the second theme that can be used to assess state actions toward localities. Targeting means that states give preferential assistance to those distressed and declining communities most in need, primarily localized in urban areas.[4] The ACIR's initial analysis indicates that even in the instances where targeting is employed, funds tend to be distributed too loosely, so that all too many of communities share in state monies. It further indicates that the majority of states have yet to develop criteria by which to identify distressed local governments, an action requisite to targeting community aid.[5]

The states appear to have rejected the concept of targeting for the concept of balanced growth—despite federal pressure to reconcile the two aims. Preliminary analysis implies that the reason for the preference of balanced growth over targeting is twofold. First, state legislatures are more favorably disposed to programs which have wide geographic appeal and where support can be more easily gathered. Second, state officials hesitate to label communities as distressed or declining for fear of offending local officials.[6]

In addition to balanced growth and targeting, there are other themes for research to consider in state dealings with metropolitan areas. First, there is the taxpayers' revolt; it is real and has its most immediate impact on local governments. What are the implications of state and local cost cutting in state dealings with metropolitan areas? Certainly, one is that the policy debate of the 1980s will be characterized by pragmatism, and programs will have to be increasingly justified on the basis of specific results rather than on that of need alone. If local governments are unlikely to float new bonds for new roads, sewers, water mains, schools, and libraries in suburban areas, will the urban sprawl at least be contained? Will the central cities of metropolitan areas become predominant ones again?

Another possible research theme is the manner in which states receive urban policy information and their capacity to deal with and manage such information. In Chap. 7, we examined selected approaches to urban and metropolitan policymaking, but we need to examine still further the types of policy information and the uses of such information.

As part of Chap. 7, we noted briefly the role of state departments of community affairs. These entities need more in-depth study. Do states relate differently to communities within and outside metropolitan areas, to large cities and small towns? Who are the major clients of departments of community affairs? Are the departments of any significance to metropolitan areas?

Just as important as state assistance to localities is the state role in determining local boundaries and functions. State actions and the evidence of the resulting impacts on local boundaries and functions vary from state to state. In some states, state-established boundary change procedures give urban fringe residents a veto over territorial governmental alterations. Other states allow annexation to cities simply as the result of passing a city ordinance. Richard Nathan indicates that the most rigorous requirements tend to be found in the Northeast, while less complex rules are found in the South and Southwest.[7] As a result, local boundaries have been virtually frozen in the long-settled areas of the Northeast, while cities in the newer metropolitan areas of the nation have tended to be successful in expanding their boundaries.

The issue of boundaries also raises the critical issue of the importance of governmental structure to meeting the needs of metropolitan areas. What is not known is how and to what extent governmental structures contribute to the cause and solution of metropolitan problems. We have proposed in this volume that the issue of structure can be assessed from both a centralization and decentralization theme. Depending upon local circumstances, both centralization and decentralization of local government are means to solving urban problems. The key issue for analysis is how local governmental structures relate to various population groupings—both at the local and the metropolitan level. Are the poor, for example, denied access to resources by the existence of local governmental boundaries? In this next decade scholars must give increased attention to the actual consequences of governmental structure on metropolitan residents. This issue must be thoroughly understood before state actions or inactions in altering procedures for governmental reform can be evaluated.

THE FEDERAL CONTEXT

The role of the states can only be understood within the context of federalism. The national government has grown enormously in recent decades, especially in its involvement with urban areas. Since the public housing legislation of 1937, the national government has been giving aid directly to local entities for numerous programs. Such direct national aid to cities was continued with the Airport Act of 1946, which funded many local airports; and with the urban renewal program beginning in 1949; and it was expanded with the later model cities programs, which gave aid to poorer communities.[8]

Currently, the two major direct federal-local assistance programs are Community Development Block Grant Programs, funded at about $4 billion annually, and the General Revenue Sharing program, which distributes funds to all general-purpose local governments. Direct federal assistance to local governments is here to stay; it is part of the contemporary picture of the federal system. The magnitude of direct federal-local assistance does not necessarily imply, however, that state governments have been deprived of the resources to shape urban America. During the last decade, the states have been able to vigorously increase their assistance to localities, but more fundamentally, they have, of course, retained the authority to influence localities, and they can do this more than the federal government can. The states exist and cannot be abolished. Now they are moving to strengthen their position vis-à-vis the federal and local governments.

Dealing with metropolitan areas necessitates strong governments at every level of a federal system. Such a "new federalism," as the ACIR succinctly puts it, must be "dedicated to balance; designed to correct structural, functional, and fiscal weaknesses; and rooted in a vital partnership of strong localities, strong states and a strong National Government."[9]

The various aspects of federalism, particularly state-local governance, reflect the basic values of the American society. Americans have a strong need for community and local government, even when it is "expensive" and "inefficient." Reformers have repeatedly been surprised when their proposals for metropolitan government have been rejected by referenda. A certain bias toward small governments seems ingrained in the American system. This condition appears to be a given in assessing how states can affect metropolitan areas. What changes are possible for restructuring local government in metropolitan areas are within the domain of the states, with consultation and direction from the localities themselves. The response of states to metropolitan areas must include issues of local boundaries and governmental structure, for otherwise the response to the metropolitan process will be fragmented and reactive to the forces of urbanization.

A new federalism, made up of strong localities, states, and federal government, would rely upon negotiation as the major mechanism for dealing with urban areas. As Neal Pierce has suggested, negotiation would open up a valuable dialogue among the levels of government which would focus upon what has been accomplished; it would include a questioning of shortcomings and a discussion of possible future courses.[10] The negotiations among the overnments would include the state legislatures, forcing them to take up the issues of metropolitan areas, city survival, and basic inequities in their states. Dialogue implies coordinated efforts among national, state, and local governments. This form of federalism places states in the central position of shaping the negotiations.

What states do not have at this juncture is a strategy or planned direction for dealing with the metropolitan process. States cannot hope to significantly affect metropolitan areas without a plan of some sort. The states would be able to greatly influence the national government and localities if they had metropolitan strategies of their own. Without such strategies, the states are in no more than a reactive position to the forces of metropolitanization and the large amounts of federal resources coming into urban areas. It is the lack of a plan or a strategy to lean upon which accounts for the seeming powerlessness of states.[11]

This "seeming powerlessness" will be put to the test in the decage of the 1980s. A number of indicators suggest that the tendency toward outward urban sprawl will decline and that many central cities will spring back with a renewed dynamism. The energy crisis is forcing American people to think seriously about the hitherto relatively unimportant costs of lengthy commuting from home to job. In addition to the constraints on increased energy usage, the fact that more than half of American women now work outside of the home means that they have less and less time to travel suburban distances. They will want to minimize community trips so that child care, shopping, and recreation are close to home. The currently perceptible trend toward "gentrification"—the invasion and remodeling of deteriorating urban neighborhoods by middle-income persons—is probably not a passing fad given the limits on gasoline consumption and the increase of women in the labor force. These people are part of a cohort of thirty- to forty-five-year-olds with sizable incomes and few or no children, who are forming smaller but more independent households and thus renewing emphasis on close-in city life.

Such rejuvenation of central cities may also be promoted by the federal government's slow movement away from policies that have hurt central areas in the past. The federal system takes a while to change, and massive change takes some time, but federal officials are aware that they have been accused of causing many urban problems with their policies. Thus it is no longer the policy of the federal government to fund projects without close consideration of possible damage to locations, and very likely we will see federal measures in the future that encourage movement back to metropolitan areas and their centers.

Thus metropolitan areas are changing and more than ever in need of a state strategy. The formulation of metropolitan strategies represents the gray area of state policies during the decade of the 1980s. Several states, including California, Massachusetts, and Michigan, have made the initial effort at developing urban strategies. Other states have considered and will likely follow this approach. As with most new state initiatives, a single or few states take the lead, with the remaining states following as the need arises or the success of the leaders becomes apparent. As of now, the initial efforts have not had sufficient political backing and resources to warrant their being classified as successful. As with most new policy directions, development of state metropolitan strategies will take time to unfold. The issue has been enjoined and documentation will be needed to determine the impact upon shaping the metropolitan process.

The states thus represent the new frontier for metropolitan research. Very little is known about what states do and with what effect from their position in the "strategic middle." Scholars have focused primary attention on national and local issues. There is no consistent theory of what states are and how they function. If they are important governmental entities, as we have contended, then they will need systematic inquiry as to how they affect and can influence metropolitan areas. We are optimistic about what states will do even though much is still in the realm of the potential. We see some basic trends in (1) an awakening awareness on the part of the state official as to the needs and concerns of metropolitan areas; (2) an increased level of expenditure for urban and local needs, with some special attention to governments in metropolitan areas; (3) more competency among state-level officials, and with that more of a tendency to experiment with innovative answers to metropolitan area questions; and (4) finally, some initial attempts at formulating strategies to deal with urban and metropolitan areas.

NOTES

1. Alan K. Campbell, "States at the Crossroads," National Civic Review 4, no. 10 (1966):554-60, 568.
2. Charles Press and Charles Adrian, "Why Our State Governments Are Sick," Antioch Review 24, no. 2 (1964):149-65.
3. Advisory Commission on Intergovernmental Relations, State Community Assistance Initiatives: Innovations of the Late 70's (Washington, D.C.: U.S. Government Printing Office, May 1979), p. 3.

4. Ibid., p. 4.
5. Ibid.
6. Ibid.
7. Richard Nathan, "Is There a National Urban Crisis?" New York Affairs 3, no. 4 (1976):15.
8. William G. Colman, Cities, Suburbs, and States (New York: Free Press, 1975), p. 323.
9. Advisory Commission on Intergovernmental Relations, Tenth Annual Report (Washington, D.C.: U.S. Government Printing Office, 1969).
10. Neal Pierce, "A Public Interest Challenge for State Investment Planning," State Planning Issues 2, no. 2 (1978):8-14.
11. Norton E. Long, "The States as Political Economies," primary paper delivered at the Smithsonian Institution, Washington, D.C., October 1978.

Index

Adams, C., 103
Adrian, C., 10
Advisory Commission of Intergovernmental Relations (ACIR), 32, 80, 81, 92, 106, 109, 138, 145, 148, 156, 158
Airport Act of 1946, 158
Allman, T. D., 5, 8
American Land Institute Model Land Development Code (ALI), 122
Annexation, 60, 66—69, 80
A-95 Planning, 122—123
Atlanta Regional Commission, 77
Authority, 63

Babcock, R. F., 120—121
Banfield, E., 8, 46
Beckman, N., 11
Biederman, K. R., 109
Bish, R. L., 79
Boezi, R., 3
Bosek, R. M., 112
Bosselman, F. P., 120—121, 123, 129
Boundaries
  adjustment boards, 80
  local, 157
Brown, J., 47

Callahan, J. J., 112
Callies, D., 123, 129
Campbell, A. K., 154
Carter, J. (President), 3
Centralization, 66—77
Cities, 2, 23—24, 28, 58—60
  concentration in 28
  defined, 2, 58
  federal aid to, 2
  functions, 23—24
  versus metro areas, 2
Coastal Zone Act, Delaware, 129
Coastal Zone Conservation Commission, 129
Colman, W., 10
Committee on Economic Development, 145, 149
Communities
  civil, 33
  federal block grants, 60
  in metro areas, 31
  relationships, 32
Community Affairs
  State Department of, 138—140
Competence Theory, 51—52
Comprehensive Planning Assistance Program, 149
Consolidation, 69—76
Cooperative Service Agreement, 81—82

Council of Governments (COG), 138
Counties, 50—61
  described, 60
  function, 60

Davies, J. C., 52
Debt
  local, 105
Decentralization, 22—23, 28, 30, 77-79
DeGrove, J., 134
Delaware Coastal Zone Act, 129
Dillion's Rule, 4, 104
Douglas Commission (National Commission on Urban Problems), 78
Downs, A., 34

Economic Development, Committee on, 145, 149
Elazar, D. J., 11, 33, 51
Euclid, Ohio Case, 121
Expenditures, 13, 95—103
Externalities, 33, 38, 118, 125

Federal
  block grants, 60
  impacts, 45
Federal Aid, 157—158
  to cities, 2
  to localities, 5
Federalism
  characteristics of, 38
  conflict, 40
  defined, 40
  dual vs. cooperative, 39
  interdependence, 41
  layer cake theory of, 39
  picket fence theory of, 39
  states pivotal role in, 42—45

[Federalism]
  underlying assumption of, 38
Fesler, J. W., 78
Fragmentation
  political, 3

Gaffney vs. Cummings, 53
General Revenue Sharing (see Revenue Sharing)
Gentrification, defined, 159
Government
  consolidation, 69—76
  functions of, 1
  intergovernmental relations, 1, 56—57
  levels, 1, 37
  organization, 2
  roles, 3
  specific purpose, 62
  territorial, 60—61
  transfer of functions, 81—82
Grant, D., 139
Grants
  federal community block, 60, 158
  incentive, 149
Grodzins, M., 5—6, 10, 41
Growth
  balanced, 155—156
  management, 123—124
  Petaluma, California city of, 123
  Ramapo, New York town of, 123
Gulick, L., 51

Hackensack Meadowlands Development Commission, N. J., 130
Hallman, H., 78
Hawaii, State Land Use Commission (SLU), 129
Highways, 137
Home Rule, 37
Housing and Urban Development, U. S. Department of (HUD), 149

Ingraham, P., 11
Intergovernmental
  dependencies, 41
  partnerships, 3
  relationships, 1
  sharing of power, 41

Kerner Commission (National Advisory Commission on Civil Disorders), 78
Kincaid, D., 114
Kolesar, J. N., 9

Land Use, 2, 117—135
  cases, 121
  Fifth Amendment of U. S. Constitution, 119—120
  policy, comprehensive, 129, 131, 134
  regulation, 120
  state, 119
  taking issue, 119—120
Las Vegas—Clark County Consolidation, 75
Legislatures, reapportioned, 53
  Gaffney vs. Cummings, 1973, 53
  Mahn vs. Howell, 1973, 53
  White vs. Weiser, 1973, 53
Little, A., 92
Local Government
  authority, 4, 30
  debt, 105
  forms and functions, 56—57
  Jefferson's Plan for Self-Government, 60
  role, 56—57
  taxing power, 104
  types, 57—58
Localities
  federal aid to, 5
  state aid to, 106—114, 137
Long, N., 82, 114

Mahan vs. Howell, 1973, 53
Martin, R. C., 3, 50
Maxey, C. C., 66
Metropolis, 2
Metropolitan areas, 2, 31, 33
  versus cities, 2
  defined, 2
  nature of, 31
Metropolitan Area Transit Authority, Washington, D. C., 63
Metropolitanization
  changing demands, 26
  core, 23
  decentralization, 22—23
  defined, 16, 25
  density of, 23
  effect of, 16
  growth, 19
  interdependencies, 22—23
  problems, 47
  process of, 16—19
  SMSA (see Standard Metropolitan Statistical Area)
  specialization of, 22—23
Meyerson, M., 46
Miami—Dade County federation, 76
Municipality
  defined, 58
  types, 58
Murphy, T. P., 27
Mushkin, S., 109

Nader, R.; Study Group, 124
Naftalin, A., 3
Nashville—Davidson County Consolidated Government, Tennessee, 75
Nathan, R. P., 103, 157, 158
National Advisory Commission on Civil Disorders (Kerner Commission), 78

166 / Index

National Commission on Urban Problems (Douglas Commission), 78
National Growth and Development 1974 Report on, 34
National Governors' Conference, 45
National League of Cities, 138
National participation, 3
National urban policy, 3, 19, 149—150
Nectow vs. City of Cambridge, 1928, 121
New Jersey—Hackensack Meadowlands Development Commission, 130
New York Port Authority, 63

Ostrom, V., 79

Participation, National, 3
Petaluma, California, 123
Pierce, N., 51
Political Fragmentation, 3
Popper, F., 124
Press, C., 10
Pressman, J., 40
Property rights, 119—120, 125, 126—128

Ramapo, New York, 123
Reform, 148, 149
Rehfuss, J., 27
Revenues, 87—95
Revenue sharing, 4—5, 158
Romney, G., 82

School Districts, 62—63
Serrano vs. Priest, 31
Shalala, D., 46
Sharkansky, I., 10

Special Districts, 57—58, 61—64
Special purpose government, 62
Spillovers (see Externalities)
Sprawl, Urban, 24, 155—156, 159
Standard Metropolitan Statistical Area (SMSA), 17—18, 26, 29, 64—65, 76, 97, 100—101
  defined, 17—18
Stanley, D. T., 103
State
  aid to localities, 106—114, 137
  constitutions, 43—44
  power, 3—4, 56
  reform, 47—49
  rights, 50—51
  tax rates, 3—4
State Commissions on Local Government (SCLG), 140—149
State Community Conservation and Development, 149
State Departments of Community Affairs, 138—140
State Land Use Commission (SLU), Hawaii, 129
Suburbs, 27, 58
  defined, 58
Swanson, T., 80
Syed, A., 42, 52

Targeting, 155—156
Taxes
  income, 94
  lids, 106
  local, 4
  property, 90—93
  sales, 93—94
  state, 4
Toronto Metropolitan Federation, 76-77
Township, 61
Twin Cities Metropolitan Council of Minneapolis—St. Paul, Minnesota, 77, 130

Unigov; Indianapolis—Marion
    County consolidation, 75
Urban areas, 1—3
    history of, 24
Urban County, 61
Urbanization, 1, 42
Urban Policy, National, 3, 19,
    149—150
Urban Problems, 4, 7—9
Urban and Regional Policy Group
    Report, 3
Urban Sprawl, 24
U.S. Conference of Mayors, 138
User Charges, 87, 95

Walker, D., 5, 11, 41
Walker, J., 11, 41
Warren, R., 79
White vs. Weiser, 53
Wildavsky, A., 40
Willbern, Y., 28, 44

Ylvisaker, P., 11

Zoning, 117, 120—122, 125, 130,
    131
Zukosky, J., 9